# ENCOUNTER

# Encounter

## A weekend with intimate strangers

# John Mann

Grossman Publishers, New York

*The 1969 New York University*
*Book Publishing Workshop*
*participated in the preparation*
*and production of this book.*

To those who have helped me to come this far

# Preface

An encounter is a conscious event. Much of the day we act from habit, filling in blank spaces, completing routines that were acquired long ago. It is rare for us to focus fully on what we are about. It takes an unusual occurrence to produce this degree of interest or involvement. To encounter we must be involved.

An encounter requires at least two elements: that which encounters and that which is encountered. It need not be two individuals. It can be one individual and an external stimulus, such as a book or a blooming flower. It can be one part of an individual relating to another part. It is, in essence, a human experience.

Further, encounter is not the elements involved but the interaction between them. It is not the man and the woman, but what happens when they meet. It is the process, not the structure. It is the current, not the stream bed. It is the reality of an event unfolding in time as it is experienced by the participants.

An encounter is very simple. It is living experience. An encounter is very subtle. It is precisely what eludes the words intended to describe it.

Robots and sleepwalkers cannot encounter. Neurotics do not encounter in areas which arouse their defenses. Those who are rigidly bound to socially approved roles do not encounter. For an encounter to occur, a person must be aware of what is happening and have the freedom to choose among alternatives.

From the individual's point of view, he may become socialized at the expense of his native responses. He becomes that which is *rewarded* and loses contact with that which he *is*. To perform effectively, he must, in a sense, avoid contact with his sensations, aspirations, and feelings. They might lead him to deviate from his established patterns.

Most democratic institutions within which individuals function are originally designed to help their members lead rich and useful lives. Unfortunately, the ideology of the founders fails to take into account the normal and inevitable tendency of any system to seek its own survival first, and the good of its constituent elements second. As with the human body, the organs are ignored unless they become diseased.

It is the individual who comes to recognize his need for encounter. The motivation must come from him in the form of a thirst for contact, experience, truth. It may seem strange to use the word "truth" in this context. But sometimes we uncover the truth only by directly approaching it. If there is a tiger lurking behind the bush we can quickly determine without any doubt at all whether it is there or not. A woman's perfume can be detected after she has left the room. The odor and what it suggests can be as real an experience as meeting the person to whom it belongs.

Any encounter involves a definite risk, since it involves contact with something that we do not control. When we experience something real we are exposing ourself to its influence. It may change us in some way. For example, you are running a risk right now. Suppose I were to abruptly turn to you and ask, "What do you want? Why are you reading this book?" What would you say? Would you have any answer or would you just mumble some socially acceptable response?

"I thought it might be interesting." "I heard about it from a friend." "I am curious about encounter groups."

The answer would not matter, but the situation itself would be changed.

The preceding should give you some taste of what is meant by an encounter. What is an encounter group? An encounter *group* consists of a group of people who want to encounter—themselves, each other, those aspects of their potentialities which they have overlooked, avoided, ignored. No one can predict beforehand just when and with whom a confrontation will occur. But it is recognized as inevitable when it occurs.

An encounter *group* is another chance. It is not a substitute for life, it is a place to learn how to live more fully. A person entering such a situation leaves behind him his customary masks. His status no longer matters. His beliefs may be questioned. His own sense of himself may shift enormously.

A single individual is limited by his own routines and his expectations of others'. However, a small group has the power to create a miniature society which can, within limits, create new rules. If the people entering into this society are seeking more direct, complete, and varied experience than they customarily have, their collective intentions can greatly increase what they feel free to do. In contrast, one person exploring new kinds of behavior is working against the weight of social expectation. If he does something trivial it will be ignored. If he violates a more serious expectation, e.g., by expressing a negative emotion to a superior, he may be in trouble.

Some speak of the encounter group experience as emotional reeducation. In this sense one is learning to recognize, experience and ultimately to control one's emotions. This is a valid view. Psychotherapy involves emotional reeducation for those whose emotional life is seriously disturbed and immature. But this is relative. Most so-called average people are emotionally still at a young age. We do not leave our youthful reactions behind so much as reject them from our awareness.

Emotional reeducation is difficult and legitimate work. Love and hate, aggression, fear and awe—basic human experiences—are powerful forces with which we rarely come to terms. We choose rather to manipulate them through a series of self-defeating defenses. To deal directly with emotion, as an electrician deals directly with current, requires courage, understanding, and a willingness to experience without censorship.

But it would be premature to conclude that the major or sole function of an encounter group is to provide psychotherapy for relatively healthy people. Psychotherapy can be the point of concentration, and many of the practitioners take this focus, but such an interpretation is not inclusive of the encounter group phenomenon.

Similarly, it is equally limited to view such groups as merely presenting an opportunity to make intense human contacts in a short period of time, though such contacts do occur. People who were strangers actually find themselves in the equivalent of a crisis situation. Real love and real hate form between them with such astonishing clarity that they would like to believe that it is artificial, though the emotion is quite real.

Further, it is inappropriate to view the experience as an opportunity to run wild. It is true that one should express everything he feels as directly and truthfully as possible, not only in words but in actions. Unless the individual feels that he can be as free as he dares, the encounter group partially fails in its purpose. However, just to be free—an enjoyable and memorable experience in itself—is neither the goal nor the function of the group. Without freedom the nature of human potential cannot be manifested, but along with the manifestation of freedom must come control. The one without the other may result in damaging aftereffects, particularly when the members leave the group and return to their normal pursuits.

Finally, it is wrong to view the group exclusively as a setting for personal revelation combining religious experience with self-confrontation. The encounter experience can occur between the individual and a cosmic power, whether nature, God, or the group, as an experience partially independent and beyond the life of the individual, but of course it is not limited to this.

It is wrong to believe that the purpose of these groups is any *single* attainment. No one really knows where an encounter can take him. All that is known is that on various occasions all of these paths, along with others that have not been mentioned, have been successfully explored. But just as we do not know what the next day will be like until we open our eyes and greet the morning, we cannot tell where an individual or group is ready to move. Our speculations and predictions often tend to block our perceptions, so that instead of perceiving *that which is,* we superimpose *that which ought to be* according to some preconceived scheme.

There are many directions for an encounter group to take. A list would include: sensory awareness, expressive movement, environmental awareness, social-emotional expression, aesthetic appreciation, intellectual problem-solving, creativity, ethical values, social sensitivity, social competence, endurance, and mystical experience. This is not an exhaustive list, but it illustrates the range of activities that can enter into an encounter experience. While it is legitimate to focus on any one of these in a particular group or workshop, it is dangerous to forget that they *all* exist and that the well-developed person is one in whom all are harmoniously cultivated. Mysticism cannot be developed at the expense of problem-solving, nor social competence at the expense of emotional freedom.

For practical reasons, many of the workshops that are offered at Growth centers and elsewhere do focus on one or more of these functions at the expense of the others. Thus a weekend may be devoted to sensory awareness (coming into closer contact with the sensations and needs of one's own organism); creativity (experiencing different approaches to the release of one's imagery and actions in a non-judgmental atmosphere); and, of course, social emotional experience with others. But these experiences are best viewed as part of a necklace. The experience itself is the string, the workshops in different areas are the jewels.

In contrast, some workshops attempt to provide the opportunity to experience most or all of these levels of human functioning so that everyone in the group is likely to be reached by *something*. If some find it difficult to talk, they may enjoy moving. If others are embarrassed by their clumsy movement, they may enjoy the experience of coming into closer contact with their own sensations. If they cannot experience their own body, perhaps they can express vivid imagery. If they cannot daydream, maybe they can paint. If they cannot paint, perhaps nonverbal communication will release the inhibitions that limit their verbal expression. Everyone has an area or areas in which they function easily and with confidence. A group experience that offers a variety of opportunities allows the individual to find a more natural vehicle for expression.

To depart from habitual patterns and enter into the unpredictable and unfolding pattern of events by which we are surrounded requires a conscious willingness on the part of the individual. It is possible to force a person to confront his experience briefly through the use of surprise, reward, threat or relaxation, but outside efforts cannot and should not go very far. The person himself must want and need the experience. Otherwise it is unfair and inappropriate to attempt to encourage him from the outside. It is also a waste of energy. Something inside a person must want to be fed, want to know, if anything significant is to happen to him.

People who deal with the nature of human potential consider energy as a key concept in their explanations of their work and their goals. Every living process requires a certain amount and kind of energy, if it is to succeed. A plant needs solar energy. A person, in addition, needs energy which he receives from other people. This is most clearly seen in babies who may die or be permanently disabled from a lack of physical human contact. But it is also true of apparently mature adults. Unfortunately, our socially guided experience tends to cut us off from our own endowments. We are taught to distrust our own vitality and to limit its expression. Every defense, every emotional tension, every situation we avoid, drains us of energy. Further, resistance itself requires energy. Our personality is in part an energy-binding system that limits our access to our own resources.

In an encounter group we can find the energies within us and around us, experience them and begin to learn to control them, rather than denying or repressing them. From this point of view any technique is appropriate if it enables us to contact either the defense limiting our energy in a particular area, or helps us to contact the energy itself so that we can experience it and learn to live with it, like an unruly animal whose existence we have denied, but who appears, nevertheless, when we finally accept the possibility of its existence.

All systems, organic or non-organic, are balances of energy. They maintain their existence through exchanges with other systems. The energy transformation in the sun provides an excess which supports organic life. Plants provide vital oxygen for animals. Organic and inorganic systems, while complete in themselves, are locked together with other systems as each uses the product which the other produces in excess.

Practitioners often use phrases such as "breaking through,"

"letting go," "allowing," or "being." All of these denote different approaches to contacting experience and the energy with which it is charged. Physics is based on the assumption that every physical substance is in one sense nothing but bound energy. Just as atomic scientists seek to identify, release, and ultimately control this energy, so does the encounter group practitioner. The analogy may seem pretentious. But it has a definite reality to those who have been through the experience in its more intense forms.

A group is a set of energy systems (individuals) who feed one another. One person working through a resistance is the pioneer for another. One person's behavior is a mirror for another. One personality gives the other what it cannot provide for itself. This is true in any group formed to meet the needs of its members; the difference in an encounter group is that the exchange is not stable. People often begin as strangers. As they begin to reveal themselves and radiate to others more of their essential nature, whether it be pure and beautiful, or foul and decayed, an accelerating process is instituted. The balance requires that all the basic elements keep increasing their radiation. Each person wishes and demands more of the other. Each move is a satisfaction and a demand. This is not the case in a stable group, and certainly not the case where an individual works alone or with a practitioner.

Now, let us return to the discussion of the alternative paths to the process which evolves in an encounter experience. Talking about it in general terms can only go so far. It is not possible to transmit the experience secondhand. I could share anecdotes, but that seems insufficient. Any encounter belongs in the present, not the past. Therefore if you are to gain a more realistic sense of what I am attempting to transmit, there is only one way to do it. We must have some experience together. On the literal level this is impossible. We are separated by time and space. Nevertheless, it is possible for me to invite you to a weekend out of time, in a place that neither of us has ever been, to share with others such an experience; not a re-creation of something I have known, or something you expect, but a new experience that will evolve as we and the others who have been invited enter it.

Every reader has the illusion that he alone reads a book, just as most writers visualize a single person as the audience. But it is not so. You are one among a number who read these words, each in a different setting. What if some of you came together in response to my invitation or driven by your own need for further contact; giving one weekend out of your life; leaving all your customary pursuits behind; forgetting all relations and coming as freshly, openly and naively as you can to the place designated?

I extend such an invitation. If you wish to come, you have only to follow the directions. We will meet on a Friday evening, this Friday evening. Tonight! . . .

# Contents

ENCOUNTER

# Friday evening

(The air is cool but not unpleasant, carrying the smell of pine trees and distant fire. How many of us are there? Ten? Fifteen? I haven't really counted. A group of strangers.

(How am I feeling? Does the atmosphere make me afraid, or bring back memories of past vacations in the mountains, walking in the woods with friends I had forgotten . . . Am I impatient to begin?

(No one seems to make any effort to be friendly. I look lonely but hide it well under a smile to no one in particular. My clothes are unpacked. There is nothing to do but wait. How did I get into this thing anyway? I am not looking to be changed. Maybe there is still time to go.

(But now the people seem to be converging on the door at the end of the lobby. There is nothing to do but follow along . . .

(The next room is empty except for a few chairs and some soft-looking rugs. I start to sit in a chair but feel conspicuous. So I sit on the floor and feel uncomfortable. A man sits down next to me. He looks angry and ill at ease. I decide to leave him alone and look around at the other people who are looking around at me. The room is getting noisier . . . Why doesn't something happen! . . .

(The leader comes in. He must have been the one pacing up and down outside. He is clearing his throat.)

"I want to welcome you to this experience. A few of you have been in encounter groups before, I think. Is that true? (Four people raise their hands.) For the rest of you it is a hearsay experience.

"Those who have been here before, forget what happened in the past. It can only limit and distort the present. For those of you who have ideas and expectations, let them go. Those of you who really don't know what to expect are in the best position.

"I don't want to talk a lot."

"So why are you?" cracks a young girl near the front.

He ignores her. "But there are one or two things I want to say, or I feel should be said. Unless others feel strongly, I shall proceed. (A gentle murmur of reactions: "Why doesn't he just get on with it . . ." "He doesn't seem too sure of himself . . ." "He is kind of cute . . .")

"We will be together for the next two full days, from tonight, through Saturday and leaving late Sunday afternoon. While we are together you have an opportunity that does not exist in the outside world. You can try out new kinds of behavior without being hurt in the process. We are all here to test limits, explore our own natures and find out in action what we are capable of achieving.

"This cannot happen by magic. Each of you must be willing to attempt to do things you would not ordinarily want to do. You must meet some of your own fears and stretch some of your muscles. Anything you get, you will pay for. Anything you want, you can achieve in some form if you really want it and are willing to submit to the uncertainty, anxiety, and effort that may be involved.

"Everyone is here, or should be here for themselves. While I have a responsibility for the over-all process, even I am here because it is a means of attaining growth for myself."

"Why should we pay for your growth?" says the outspoken young woman.

"You shouldn't, Penny. You should pay for your own. If each of you could find opportunities under normal social conditions to grow, experiment and experience as freely as you need, you wouldn't be here. But those opportunities are rare. You should be here because you need to be. You may not realize it at this point. By Sunday afternoon it will be clearer . . .

"What is it that you would like to achieve or experience while you are here? I am not asking you to say out loud. Just come to a definite conclusion for yourself."

(A minute of deep silence ensues. I am thinking. Nothing seems to come. What am I supposed to want? It would be easier if it were going to be made public. I have a pretty good idea what he wants me to want. What is the leader's name anyway? Richard. I wonder what people call him . . . But what do I want? It would be nice to feel happy, but that doesn't seem adequate . . . I would like to face something about myself . . . But what . . . I don't know. That sounds so therapeutic . . . I guess what I would really like to know, what I would really like to sense, is the nature of my capacities! What I could become.)

"All right. Now I give you another task. Decide for yourself what you are most afraid might happen to you during the weekend. Again keep it to yourself. But decide on something definite and real."

(The silence this time is different. It has an ominous quality. I am afraid that everyone will suddenly start staring at me accusingly. I am afraid people will find out that I am just curious and get angry at me. No, no, that is all trivial. I am afraid of being found out. I guess that is it. But about what? By whom? I don't know. But that is the feeling. I have had it before . . .)

"At certain moments you will be faced with a choice. At those points you will either press on regardless of uncertainty or fear, or you will give up and begin to run. What you do will be crucial. Nothing can be decided beforehand, however. If you find it in you to keep moving, then you can break through into an important experience. I hope that you will. We all have a stake in one another, even though we are strangers. Everyone who falters affects all the rest. Any success is shared. Work for yourself but realize that in a deeper sense we all are tied together.

"Let us try a simple experiment . . . Everyone form a circle . . . sit comfortably as you can and join hands."

(My feet are a little stiff, but it is a relief to be doing something concrete.)

"I am going to say a few things as we hold hands together but I ask the rest of you to remain quiet until we are finished.

"There is nothing that has to happen. There is nothing to do but experience being in this room sitting down, holding hands . . . How do the hands feel? Are they both the same?"

(The woman on my right has a small sweaty cold hand. The man on my left has a large, rough hand.)

"Become aware of the breathing of the person on each side of you . . . Don't change your own, just sense theirs . . ."

(I hadn't heard them breathe before. I can see their chests move. We seem to be breathing in the same rhythm.)

"Stay with the awareness. Don't force anything. Don't try to breathe as they are breathing. Just let your breath do what it wants to do . . . Relax . . . Be aware of what is happening . . . Let go."

(I am feeling heavier, sinking into the floor. I feel more at ease holding these hands. It is comforting to be in contact with the whole group . . . as long as no one lets go. It would be nice to sleep holding hands like this . . .)

"Now become aware of your own organism as the center from

which every impression radiates . . . Sense your own breathing
. . . your own heartbeat . . . the movement in your eyes . . .
Just sink into these inner rhythms that go on without you . . ."

(I am sitting here, feeling more and more like a kaleidoscope
of inner images and less and less like a person. It is very pleasant
but it is a little scary.)

"Sense whether you give off any energy. Do you feel warmth
within you? Do you radiate it into the atmosphere . . . to the
people around you? . . . Become aware of your right hand. Feel
the energy in your right hand. Don't strengthen your grip, just
feel your energy. Feel it throbbing. Feel the blood moving, the
muscles . . . the bones . . . the tendons. Let the energy from
your body enter your right hand . . . Let it leave your hand and
enter the hand you are holding . . . It goes from you into the
chain of arms. It passes from one person to the next."

(It must be suggestion. But I can feel something being given
off. I guess it is just body heat.)

"Put your attention on your left hand . . . What do you receive from the person on your left? . . . Can you sense beyond
him to the person on his left? . . . Can you sense the full circle,
the force leaving you on your right and returning on your left?
I am going to be quiet for a minute or two. Experience the circle
. . . the breathing . . . your own energy . . . the force moving
around the group. When you have had enough, let go."

(Silence. Thoughts keep coming into my mind . . . Images
from traveling . . . little worries . . . But I am sitting here
. . . quietly waiting, content . . . I am a little stiff, but I don't
want to move. It really feels good. I feel stronger. I don't know
why. It is spooky. I can feel something leaving my right and
something returning on my left, like a faint echo . . . The longer
I sit here the better I feel . . . It is as if I were plugged into a
battery. I can close my eyes and just be here . . . quietly gain-
ing strength . . . as if I were sun-bathing or walking in a gentle

rain . . . people are breathing on either side of me . . . what a
relief not to know who they are . . . not to have to relate, but
just to share . . . without words . . .

(But I almost feel that I should end it . . . as if it were too soon
. . . Why should I feel so good without knowing anyone? . . .
maybe if I knew who they were and how they were feeling, I
wouldn't be so at ease . . . But as long as it lasts I am safe
. . . everyone is touching so no one can do anything to me. They
can't touch me and they can't hit me . . . and I can't touch them
. . . Maybe that is why people shake hands . . .

(I keep thinking and thinking . . . Why can't I stop and just
enjoy being here? I don't think it will last much longer . . . a
few people are getting restless . . . Richard is looking
around . . .)

"Remain just as you are. Don't stop whatever is happening.
But when you have had enough, open your eyes, if they are
closed, and then look around you at the other members of the
group as you let go of the hands on either side of you. Take all
the time you want."

One by one, like a dissolving chain, the group members open
their eyes and release hands, each in a different style; abruptly,
reluctantly, slightly embarrassed or quietly. They look at each
other with a slight sense of wonder.

Richard: What do you see? How do you feel about one another?

—Everyone looks so much more vivid, in three dimensions.

—I feel sad. I lost something when I let go of the other
hands.

—I feel just the same.

—I feel like I just woke up from a dream. Am I supposed to
feel that way?

Richard: There is no right or wrong. For myself I feel much

closer to you. Before a group begins, I usually feel nervous and detached. That is gone.

—I feel more comfortable too, as if we all knew each other somewhere else before we came here. It feels like a class reunion.

—I am irritated. Why I don't know.

Richard: At yourself or someone in the group?

—At myself, at the group, at you.

Richard: All for the same reason?

—I resent being made to feel inadequate. I didn't experience anything at all. Before, I was all right. Now I am peculiar. Do I lack something or are you all kidding yourselves? I have heard groups are just great emotional blood baths.

Richard: At the moment you seem to be the one who is expressing the strongest emotion.

—I don't feel like he does, but I can understand it. (Why did I have to open my big mouth?)

Richard: Would you two mind sitting in the center of the group and talking to each other?

—Why do we have to sit in the center? Why can't we stay where we are! I don't like being manipulated!

Richard: If you only do what you like, you will never get anywhere. Do it as an experiment. If it doesn't work, what have you lost?

—My self respect . . . But all right. You're the leader. If that's the way you do things . . . (He sure is a stubborn character. What difference does it make where we sit? But I certainly feel conspicuous.)

—So you think you understand how I feel?

—Yes. But you don't have to sound as if you were accusing me of a crime.

—I'm sorry. I feel on the defensive in front of all these people . . . as if I were a little boy who had been caught doing something wrong.

—You don't have to feel that way.

Richard: Let us change the situation a little bit. What is your name?

—My name is Frank.

Richard: And what is yours?

—Mine? Marcia.

Richard: Frank, can you remember an actual situation in which you felt the way you just described, as if you were a little boy caught doing something wrong?

Frank: I suppose so, but what is the point?

Richard: Describe it.

Frank: Do I have to? I think this is ridiculous.

Marcia: Go on, Frank. (It's funny. I feel so much closer to him sitting here.)

Frank: Well, the thing that pops into my head first is one time when I was about seven and I had taken some apples from a neighbor's orchard, and he had called my mother and . . .

Richard: (interrupting) Could Marcia be your mother?

Frank: She doesn't look like her.

Richard: Is there any similarity?

Frank: A little bit.

Richard: Are you willing to try?

Marcia: If I have to. Couldn't someone else do it better? (How the hell did I get myself into this?)

Richard: I honestly don't know. But you are there. You have heard that your son has been stealing apples. Go ahead.

Marcia: . . . Well, son, what have you been up to this morning?

Frank: (looking afraid and defiant) Nothing!

Marcia: That isn't what I heard.

Frank: I'll bet that louse Mr. Robbins has called you. All I did was take three.

Marcia: Apples?

Frank: Yes.

Marcia: Do you think that was the right thing to do?

Frank: What difference do three apples make?

Marcia: One apple can make a lot of difference.

Frank: (*to Richard*) She didn't say that.

Richard: But Eve did. Just go on.

Frank: I didn't mean no harm. He doesn't pick them anyway. All the kids eat them. Nobody yells at them.

Marcia: I'm not yelling. I don't care what most kids do. They are his apples and his trees and you have no right to eat them unless he says it is all right.

Frank: All right. All right.

Richard: How are you feeling right now?

Frank: I feel angry and little. I am sorry I took the apples but I don't want to admit it. Why doesn't Mommie understand!

Richard: How do you feel, Mother?

Marcia: I don't like to be stern, but he has to know right from wrong. Next time it will be somebody's clothes and later an automobile.

Frank: She wouldn't think that. She would think, "He is going to be just like his brother Herbie, a nogoodnik."

Richard: How does this end?

Frank: I promise not to do it any more and to apologize to Mr. Robbins.

Richard: Have you had enough of this, or do you want to go on?

Frank: Where is there to go to? It all seems a little silly. It was long ago and I had forgotten all about it.

Richard: You didn't answer my question.

Frank: If you think it will do any good. But I'm sure everyone is bored.

Richard: (*to group*) Are you bored?

—No.

—I'm curious to find out what you have in mind.

—I'm glad if you focus on him. It leaves me out of it.

Richard: Your time will come.

—Is this how we are going to spend our time? It seems stupid!

Richard: What is your name?

—Thurston P. Dartworth!

Richard: Well, Thurston. What do they call you for short?

Thurston: My associates call me "Thirsty."

Richard: What irritates you about this situation, Thirsty?

Thurston: (*irritably*) Did I say I was irritated! Who cares about that little mama's boy?

Richard: Could you be Herbert?

Thurston: What!

Richard: You know, Frank's brother. Could you talk to him like a brother? Tell him a few things about the way of the world.

Thurston: I don't know what his brother was like, but I sure could put that little snot-nose kid straight in a hurry.

Richard: Is that all right with you, Frank?

Frank: Yeah, he has the same expression.

Richard: All right, Marcia, why don't you move aside and let Herbert step in.

(Why do I feel disappointed? I should be relieved.)

Richard: Tell us a little about Herbert.

Frank: He was my older brother. He is the black sheep of the family.

Richard: Why?

Frank: He got into some trouble. He was always getting into trouble. He was three years older. I remember talking to him. I don't know if it was after stealing the apples, but it was around that time. He came over and started asking questions about what happened.

Thurston as Herbert: I hear you got caught in the orchard.

Boy, that was stupid! I've been getting apples from old man Robbins for years and never gotten caught.

Frank: I forgot where I was and when I looked up there he was.

Herbert: I don't know how you're ever going to amount to much if you can't look both ways. Hell, Frank, you really are stupid. You know that.

Frank: Oh, shut up. (*to Richard*) Then he told me about something he had planned.

Richard: Reverse roles then. You become your brother and Thurston will be you.

Frank as Herbert: Just to show that I'm a good guy and not always tearing you down, I'll let you in on something.

Thurston as Frank: Oh yeah, what?

Frank as Herbert: I'm going into the old Winthrop house.

Richard: All right, Frank, be yourself again.

Frank: The Winthrop house? Are you crazy? That place is supposed to be haunted. And the police keep an eye on it. What do you want to go there for?

Herbert: That's where I'm going. I don't have to explain it to you. Do you want to come with me or not?

Frank: No . . . I know you think I'm scared, but suppose you get caught? You could get in real trouble.

Herbert: Oh, the hell with you. This is your last chance. (*pause*) No? All right. See you around. (*He gets up and leaves.*)

Richard: What happened to Herbert?

Frank: He got caught. I remember the police coming. But that was nothing compared to what happened when he was fourteen. You want to hear about that?

Richard: I'm not sure. How are you feeling? At the beginning you were very reluctant to start. Now you seem to want to go on.

Frank: I feel different. All of these things which I haven't

(Now I'm going to hit him in the tummy . . . he is like a big man doll that I can play with . . . I'm going to muss up his hair . . . and make little pigtails . . . My, does he look cute . . . Now I'll put his arms up straight in front of him . . . and walk into them . . . and lick his face . . .)

Richard: Five minutes are up. You can talk to each other.

Silence.

Marcia: You are a great big teddy bear.

Frank: You are an overgrown feminine tomboy.

Marcia: I want to hug you again.

Frank: Come here.

Marcia: That's nice. (I must be making a fool of myself.)

Richard: What are you thinking, Marcia?

Marcia: I am thinking that I must be making a fool of myself.

Richard: Frank, is she making a fool of herself?

Frank: If she is, I enjoy it.

Marcia: I don't mean with him . . . with the group.

Richard: You have all been quiet for a long time. What reactions are you having?

—I envy her. Everything seems so easy. I could never express anything like that in the middle of a group. I get embarrassed just thinking about it.

—I am a little reluctant to say anything. It seems to me that what they do is their business.

Richard: Don't talk about them, talk about yourself. How do you feel? Does it all remind you of anything in your own experience?

—I don't really want to go into it. But I can tell you how I feel—sad. I'm not sure why. It isn't for them. It's for myself. I'm not so old, only twenty-six, but my life feels old.

—You look as if you might cry.

—I wish I could. I don't know if it would do any good but it would be a relief. But I haven't cried in a long time, and I am not about to right now. I have forgotten how.

Richard: Anyone else?

—Is there something wrong with me? I think they are very shallow and exhibitionistic. I don't mean to be nasty, but we are supposed to tell the truth!

Richard: How do you feel about me?

—You seemed to get a lot of satisfaction from manipulating people.

Richard: Anyone else you have a kind word for?

—I must say that question irritates me. I just feel uncomfortable with all these people who seem upset, or admire what a wonderful thing Frank and Marcia are experiencing.

Richard: Does anyone want to respond to that?

Frank: I do. I can understand how he feels. It sounds like I felt before I got involved. I suppose from the outside it could look as if I had been manipulated into something I didn't want or need. But it isn't so. I can feel now that I was asking for it. When I attacked Richard, it was my way of finding out something about him. I have been led, but I needed leading. I know it may seem superficial and hard to accept, but as I look at Marcia now, who was a total stranger an hour ago, I feel a warmth and a relationship that seems very real.

(When he glances at me, I can feel the warmth in my heart.)

Frank: It feels like we are playmates. I don't know what she will do next or she me. That is a feeling I haven't had in a long time. And there is no socialized obligation, which is one hell of a relief . . .

(Why does a pang of disappointment hit me when he says that?)

Frank: That's how it is to me. All I can hope is that you get involved as things go along and get a taste of it for yourself.

Richard: Anyone else?

—I have been sitting here thinking about my brother Ben. He was younger. I always used to kid with him and make fun of him. I haven't seen him in five years. I am just wondering whether I had more of an effect on him than I realized. If he was trying to copy me, he sure didn't do a very good job, or else I set a lousy example. I wish I could talk to him and find out.

Frank: What is stopping you?

—He is dead. He was killed in the war. So it doesn't really matter to him any more.

Richard: But it matters to you.

—Yes, I guess it does. But why haven't I realized it before? Why does it take a stranger to make me begin to realize it? Oh, hell . . . I guess I didn't want to remember. He was such a crazy kid. I was crazy too, but I knew what I was doing. He was just crazy. If he only knew when to hide and when to run across a field where the bullets were flying. He only knew how to run. Stupid kid.

—Are you finished? I don't want to interrupt.

—What is there to say?

—Well then, I am sitting here thinking of an argument I had with my mother a year ago. I hadn't been home in a long time. I haven't been there much in the last five years. It was a bad scene . . .

Richard: You want to say any more?

—No.

Silence.

—I'm sorry. I just can't be quiet. I think it is a lot of crap. Everybody is just hypnotizing themselves, dredging up things out of their past and getting emotional.

Richard: What would you suggest?

—That we act like mature human beings. Of course we all

have unresolved experiences, but do we have to slobber all over everybody else? Can't we approach these things intelligently?

Richard: What is your name anyway?

—Thomas.

Richard: Why don't you pick someone out, Thomas, and have an intelligent conversation with them for a few minutes?

Thomas: You can call me Tom. I doubt if anyone here would want to have an intelligent conversation with me.

Richard: Well, that is up to them, but regardless of how they respond, at least you can have one with them and illustrate to us what you are talking about. So be courageous, even if it seems stupid. Pick someone out and we will all sit around you and listen.

Thomas: All right. I'll pick you. What's your name?

—My name is Restas. To save you the next question, I am from an occupied country in Europe that has ceased to exist. Let's let it go at that.

Thomas: I am not interested in being personal. Let me just ask you as an intelligent grown-up adult, how does all this strike you?

Restas: I am not sure. It reminds me of some experiences that I have had in Europe, but they had a cultural flavor which this lacks. It is not so difficult for me to let go as it seems to be for you.

Thomas: Doesn't this all seem like some cultish experience? Someone pushes the button and emotions come out. I find it offensive.

Restas: Isn't someone always pushing a button everywhere, at work, at home? Every habit, every rule, every social expectation is a button. Maybe you picked the wrong person to talk to. I am somewhat disturbed about American culture. It is rich in opportunities but rather superficial. And persons like you are far too wrapped up in ideas that have little reality. Have you ever worked with your hands? Have you ever really been hungry?

Thomas: Yes, but not for long. I suppose it was too much to expect that I would find a sensible adult in this crowd. You are all overgrown children.

Restas: If we are, that makes you a premature adult. But I don't think it is that simple. You seem to me very tight in the head. I have the feeling that there is a restriction in your upper neck to keep out emotions. Your face has a very tight expression. Have you ever cried?

Thomas: Have I ever what! Is this intellectual?

Restas: You can be intellectual. I will be what I want.

Thomas: I want an intelligent exchange.

Restas: Let me propose a question for discussion. How can two people understand what it means to touch without touching?

Thomas: I don't want to touch anyone. In fact, I am thankful that no one has got it into their heads to touch me yet.

Restas: You don't like to be touched?

Thomas: It gives me an uncomfortable feeling, like being caught in a spider web. I simply want to get away when it happens.

—It sounds like a hang-up.

Thomas: Now that is precisely the kind of stupid remark that really makes me angry! Such a dull, stereotyped, unthinking statement.

—You are really reacting. I must have hit the nail on the thumb.

Thomas: Everyone has "hang-ups." Everyone has difficulties. So what! It proves nothing except that I am human. And why must I like to be touched? . . . That is another thing that I find objectionable, the tyranny of the group. I have the definite impression, even though it is too soon to be sure, that there are a whole series of assumptions made by you people to which one is expected to adhere, or else be rejected.

Richard: That is an interesting statement. Could you be more specific?

Thomas: I would be delighted. First, everyone is supposed to love one another or, if not love, at least be physically demonstrative. It doesn't matter what you feel as long as it is strong. Let me see . . . Second, you are supposed to tell the truth, which seems to mean to say all the nasty things you would ordinarily think but not express . . . And third, you cannot sit back and observe but must be involved in some mystical thing called the "group process"—though what that is, I don't know. And fourth, . . . you are supposed to go through some great experience and come out different than when you began, something in the nature of a conversion. And fifth, . . . let me see, fifth, you are supposed to look to the leader as some kind of Western style guru who guides, participates, but does not really get involved. He legitimizes whatever happens, as long as he approves of it. He is a kind of beneficent ideal image to which we are supposed to aspire . . . Let me see . . . sixth . . .

Restas: I am very interested in what you say. As you might expect, I am rather sensitive to any totalitarian situation, whether of a government or a group, having lived through several of such experiences in Europe. I do not agree that these five rules actually exist or, if they do, I believe they could be altered without too much difficulty. But whether you want to or not, your very suspiciousness and hostility has helped me and, I suspect, others, to be on guard against certain dangers that can overtake us . . . But there is one principle, perhaps more important than any you mentioned, which you have not mentioned. Whether it is practiced here it is too soon to judge, but I have become convinced of its importance through personal experience in other contexts. It is that everything, no matter how private or sacred, is open for public inspection and discussion. That is the best protection I know. Insidious, evil, and perverse things grow

in secrecy. They shrivel up in the light of day. I don't care so
much what people do as whether they are willing to expose it
and live with the consequences.

Thomas: You are more radical than I am. I don't know that I
want to expose anything or everything. That makes me think of
a sixth principle. "You are supposed to make some kind of con-
fession of a personal nature." It all feels to me a little like brain-
washing. I just don't like it.

Restas: What do you propose to do?

Thomas: What can I do? Make the best of it, I suppose. I could
leave. That was my first reaction. But why should I allow myself
to be driven away by something just because I don't believe in
it or am afraid of it?

Restas: Of what are you afraid?

Thomas: Are you serious? I keep expecting to be told to do
some "encountering," to touch someone or share some personal
experiences, to wallow in emotions.

Restas: But it hasn't happened.

Thomas: Not yet, but it will. It must. It is like a lynching party.
If the crowd is prepared and the rope is ready, somebody must
be hung. If the prisoner escapes, then any convenient deviant
will do.

Richard: If you truly want to be left alone, the cruelest thing
I could do to you in your present state is to accept your wish.
However, think about the possibility that everything you say
may be an elaborate defense against experiencing some of the
things you have been describing. Why did you come here if you
were not looking for something of this nature? Surely you didn't
expect a forum discussion.

Thomas: I no longer remember.

Richard: Why don't you move back in the circle where you
can feel safer? But think about one thing, Thomas, since you

are so enamored of thought: there is no point in being here unless you experiment with new kinds of behavior. Each person must sooner or later face the choice of doing precisely that which they want to avoid. If they find it in them to move ahead in spite of their fear, something unexpected and meaningful is possible. If they side-step or avoid the possibility, it is a lot of play-acting and stereotyped behavior like any other life experience. Each of us, including myself, will have to make the choice, probably at different moments.

—Is it too late to bring something up? Everyone must be very tired.

Frank: I'm tired, but I don't think I could sleep. Who are you and what's on your mind?

—I'm Ann. And I'll tell you what is on my mind. It is funny that you should be the one to ask.

Frank: So tell me already.

Ann: You just make me furious, that's all.

Frank: Me? I don't even know you. I haven't even noticed you . . . No. That isn't true. I felt that you were looking at me a couple of times.

Ann: I don't know what it is, but every time you open your mouth, I would just like to belt you one. That isn't very ladylike. And if I did, I think you would look at me with a tolerant sneer on your lips and a pitying expression . . . You can't believe that anyone could possibly have that reaction to you, could you!

Frank: I don't know what to think. Do we really have to go into this? Does it have anything to do with me?

Richard: There are several ways we could approach this situation. We could find out whom you remind Ann of; she could have the opportunity of expressing her feelings by hitting Frank or yelling at him or whatever she felt. But I want to suggest something simpler and more naive.

Frank: What is that?

Richard: That you both get up, go to different ends of the room, look at one another and then slowly walk together.

Ann: Nothing more?

Richard: If you try it, you will find that it can be quite a lot.

Ann: I'm game.

Richard: Well, if you both are, then get up and move to opposite corners of the room . . . that's right . . . now look at each other and as slowly as you want, walk together . . . not too fast . . . take all the time you need . . . look at each other, not past each other . . . that's right . . . don't talk . . . and when you come together, then do whatever feels natural . . . but no words . . . stay with it as long as you have anything to do . . .

(I am very tense . . . Is she going to wallop him? . . . I am afraid she might . . . She looks so angry and intent . . . and he doesn't seem to care . . . or maybe he doesn't realize . . . God, it is quiet . . . My right arm is clenching so tight, it hurts . . . I don't want her to hit him . . . but I hope she does . . . Don't just stand there . . . Come on, Frank, do something . . . Don't just wait . . . She really is making him sweat . . . walking around him . . . stalking him . . . It's lucky he can't see how she looks . . . It must be hard to have someone who is hostile standing behind your back . . . but he won't move . . . What kind of an idiot is he? . . . maybe he thinks she won't touch him if he does that . . . He doesn't know women . . .

(Oh, wow! Wow! . . . It's lucky she hit him in the shoulder . . . Boy, she really means it . . . He just stands there, taking it . . . maybe it doesn't really hurt . . . he looks like it hurts . . . Oh, that's better. He has stopped her . . . Boy, now she is really angry . . .)

Ann: (*screaming*) You god damn son of a bitch! I want to kick you in the balls.

(He just looks at her . . . I guess I'd be puzzled too . . . It seems to be over . . . The words broke the spell . . . I feel better . . . I wonder how he feels?)

Richard: What is going on in you, Ann?

Ann: What? I'm sorry. I didn't hear you.

Richard: I said, "What are you experiencing inside yourself?"

Ann: I am shaking just like a leaf. I'm still angry, but I am afraid too.

Richard: Would you like to be held?

Ann: Not by him.

Richard: No, not by him . . . Now, is that better? (*He holds her.*)

Ann: I feel safer, but I am still shaking.

Richard: Shake all you want. Don't hold anything back. If you want to cry or scream, just let it come.

Ann: I wouldn't give him the satisfaction.

Richard: You wouldn't give whom?

Ann: Just hold me and stop asking so many questions.

Richard: I'm not so sure I want to.

Ann: Just like a man. If you don't do what he wants, he pushes you away.

Richard: I'm still here. You want me to say I want to if I don't.

Ann: You're not supposed to be a human being. You just give me what I need.

Richard: (*stepping back*) Why the hell should I?

Ann: That's what you're paid to do, isn't it? So come back here and do it.

Richard: I wouldn't touch you with a ten-foot pole.

Frank: You want me to hold you?

Ann: Stay away from me, you fink.

Frank: I think I will. All you can do is hit me again. I want to. (*He approaches her.*)

Ann: Some people don't learn. Don't worry. I'm not going to

hit you, but don't expect me to fall passionately into your arms, you imbecile.

Frank: (*coming closer*) You remind me of my baby sister. She used to throw things at me. Once she threw a book end and split my scalp. Boy, what a mess . . . Now, is that so horrible?

Ann: When you are near me, I just go mushy all over. It feels like a strange tropical disease.

Frank: I don't believe it. You feel warmer. You just haven't the honesty to admit it . . . Hell, I don't know who you take me for and I don't care, but whoever it is, it isn't me. Can't you begin to realize that?

Ann: Somehow I don't want to realize it. I wish I had you wired to some great electric machine and whenever I wanted, I could throw the switch and watch you jump. That I would enjoy. I wish you had a battery and whenever I wanted, I could reach into a compartment in your back and take it out. Then you would stop dead until I decided, in my own good time, to put it back in. That would really be fun.

Frank: Are you feeling better?

Ann: I am feeling fine. I wish you were a puppet with seven different strings and I could stand up there on a platform and make you do anything I wanted, and then at the end I would come out and take a bow and everyone would say, "Why, it is a woman."

Frank: Well, I am glad that I stimulate such fantasies. I didn't think women went in for this kind of thing.

Ann: Actually, what I would really like to do is to tie you to a bed and . . . (*pause*)

Frank: And then what?

Ann: Oh, I have to stop somewhere.

Richard: You are just getting interesting.

Ann: That's tough. I've had enough. I'm going to bed. Anyone coming? (*She pauses briefly and then leaves.*)

Richard: Anyone need to say anything pressing?

Marcia: Is that all for tonight?

Richard: Isn't it enough? Tomorrow may be a very long day. Don't stay up all night talking or drinking. Get some sleep.

Thomas: When is breakfast?

Richard: You will find an announcement in your room covering all that kind of information.

Penny: Does anyone want to take a short walk? I'm too restless to sleep . . . Do you, Thurston? . . . (*They leave.*)

(I don't look at anyone. I have had it. I go right to my room.)

# Friday night

(I want to lie down. I want to go blank, but I feel like a tense violin.

(Maybe I should take a bath. But I don't want to take a bath. I want to run or walk. But I am too tired. I want to go to sleep. But I can't sleep. Oh hell!

(I feel lonely. I wonder if anyone is around. Boy, am I acting like a hysterical female. Just calm down, Marcia. Sit by the window, look at the stars and breathe deeply.

(It is so dark out there. No moon at all . . . a few stars through the trees. I remember when I was five years old, sitting on the floor looking out the window and wondering what it was like to die. Thinking and thinking about it until the darkness outside began to enter the room and I got scared. I have always been afraid of the dark. Not because I couldn't see. I don't mind not being able to see, but because I might disappear in the dark. I wonder if I have always been this morbid.

(I get so sick of myself. I wish that I could go to sleep and wake up a different person, with a new memory. But I would have to know that it wasn't me. If I couldn't remember that I was really myself there would be no point to it.

(I need a sweater. The room is chilly. The wind is trying to get through the window. I'll put on my warm woolly sweater with red and gray stripes, open the window wide and let it all come in.

(The window is stuck. It hasn't been opened in a long time. But I'm going to get it. I'm going to push it until . . . That's better. The air is laden with pine resin. It would be nice to sleep outside. I'll just stay up here and look down, watch and listen.

(It is so quiet. The wind has hidden itself away. I can almost feel the pressure of the starlight. I wish I could go to sleep. What is keeping me awake? I am only going to be exhausted to-morrow. It is so stupid . . .

(The wind is beginning to pick up now. It touches me, moves around me and through me. It doesn't know who I am. It doesn't care where I have been, whom I know, what I have done. It accepts me, caresses me, cools me and passes on.

(I would like to float on the wind. To be carried wherever it wanted to go and not come down all night . . .

(I am hungry for something. I want to bite into something; not food, but some experience. I want to fight some resistance, break into something. I want to be free. I want to run through the forest and cry out. But I won't. I am afraid people would think I was crazy and I wouldn't want to wake anyone up.

(I wonder what it would be like to sleep with Frank? Now where the hell did that thought come from? I don't think I would want to. I don't want anyone around. I need to get away. But still it would be good to be held all night long . . .

(I am really scared. Something inside is trembling. What is there to tremble about? Maybe I should shut the window. I must be over-tired.

(I am a silly girl on her first night away from home. And I am homesick. But for what? For a home that is destroyed and exists only in my memory.

(I am beginning to feel haunted. There are people in this

room . . . my parents, sister, friends . . . the dark walls are getting lighter and turning into screens on which I can project forgotten images. I am too tired to resist and too egotistical to be indifferent. Maybe after it is over I can fall asleep.

(They are all ghosts . . . my mother who has been dead five years, my sister who lives 250 miles away, Michael who has gone away—they are each saturated with emotional dew which I have put on them. I am bemused by their existence. They affect me but they cannot hurt me now. I am enchanted. They are in my mind. I control them. If they come too close I can blur their image. If they start to fade I can recall them by conjuring up a detail; a gesture with the hand while smoking, a nervous expression of the lips . . . and they return . . .

(My whole life waits offstage. I do not have time and am too vigilant to allow it to appear ordinarily. But tonight I am off guard and worn down. And there it is, as if it waited for the right conditions, like a full eclipse of the sun.

(And then there is the encounter group. Those people. So intense, some so frightened, so defensive. And myself getting caught up in that tide of activity. Not knowing where it goes.

(Why am I afraid to sleep? Am I afraid or is it just excitement? . . . I am out of control. I am disturbed. Maybe I am crazy. Now that is an amusing thought. Level-headed Marcia, a coo-coo. Wouldn't that be a riot! I get back after the weekend and they ask me at the office what I got out of it and I smile sweetly and say, "Oh, I learned that I am crazy." It might be worth doing, just to see the effect. But they would only say, "Oh, we knew that all the time."

(Maybe I am crazy. What is "crazy"? Who knows what is underneath everything I keep so carefully controlled? Maybe I have a demented uncle locked in the cellar of my brain. I don't really believe it, but sometimes I can almost hear the knocking, someone shouting far away.

(Just keep it up, Marcia. You really will have yourself in a fine state. One thing I can say for you. You are suggestible. If you could only suggest yourself to sleep.

(I wonder how many other people are pacing back and forth right now. Maybe I'm the only one. The nighttime is for sleeping. What good ever came out of thinking and thinking in the dark? But I am stuck here. I don't really want to see anybody else. I'm beginning to be afraid that they would look at me and say, "Boy, do you look scared or crazy." That would be all I need. But it would be nice to pound on the walls and yell "Fire, Fire" as loud as I could. Then maybe I could go to sleep. Or how about "Help, help, I am being attacked by a castrated communist spy." That would stir things up for a few minutes.

(I wonder if this place is a firetrap. It seems all made of wood, except for the fireplaces. I could always jump out the window. It would really be nice to watch this place burn down. I could absolutely enjoy that, watching the great flames and the eerie shadows they cast into the forest, and feeling the warmth from a safe distance. And after a little while it would start to rain and put out the embers and save the forest. I would need to save the forest. Smokey the Bear would be angry if I didn't save the forest.

(What has gotten into me? This could go on and on. I could be a big black bear in the forest, crashing through the underbrush, letting out loud roars when I wanted to, or low growls . . . and rolling on the pine needles . . . and climbing trees . . . that would really be great . . . Climbing up a great old tree with sticky sap running from cracked limbs . . . growling at the crescent moon and sniffing for honey while the bees are asleep . . . Never having to go to work. I would really like to be an animal . . . Why do I have to be a person? . . .

(Marcia, you are an animal. You are a two-footed female animal with a lot of illusions and a bag full of memories, most of which only hold you back. There ought to be a bank that rents safe deposit boxes for memories. You could just leave them there, forget about them, but pick them up when you wanted them.

(I wish it would rain. I would like to watch the water streak the windowpane. I would like to hear the sound against the house and on the ground. I want it to get completely black so that I can see nothing and hear only the sound of the rain or the wind blowing the rain. I would sit here with my arms hugging my knees and feel safe, warm, and excited.

(My God, it is raining. Isn't that incredible! I must have heard it start without realizing. Or did I feel something in the atmosphere and respond to it?

(How many storms I must have seen. But this one seems realer and stranger. As if it were an unprecedented event. As if it rained once a century and only I knew that it was happening. Only I was seeing it and hearing the raindrops tapping like little elves on the window. I will not let them in. They might be devils, looking like elves. No. The rain cleanses. I will let it fall on me. Later I can change my clothes. Right now, I am going to stick my head out the window and get soaked to the skin . . .

(Wow! That is something . . . a cold sprinkly towel all over me . . . Now I'll never go to sleep. But I have to get all these clothes off . . . And I need to get warm. Where is that big towel? . . . I am just going to rub myself hard . . . I want to turn on the light, stand in front of the mirror and look at myself . . .

(There I am. I must be really flipping my lid . . . I look pretty good, like a wet mouse . . . No, that isn't so. I really look beautiful. If I were a man, I would be attracted. Of course there is a lot wrong, but it is a nice body. Hello, Marcia. There you are. You don't look the way I think you look. You probably don't feel as I would expect you to feel.

(I wonder what it would be like to make love in front of a

mirror? Something like making love in front of a group? I wonder whether there is anything to those rumors you hear about mass orgies in encounter groups? I must ask Richard how he feels about nude encounter groups . . .

(I wish I had brought a bottle of whiskey. It would warm me up and put me to sleep. If all this were only serving some purpose, other than exhausting me. I am going to be a wreck tomorrow. Just a little sleep. That isn't very much to ask . . .

(The rain seems to have stopped. I am going to strip off the linen and blankets, wrap myself up and sit by the window until I get sleepy or until I get bored.

(All I need is a campfire and a peace pipe and my hair in a long braid. They could call me Squaw Marcia Rain On Face or Little Bear Up All Night.

(The last time I was up like this was when I had a tooth extracted. I wish the hell I had brought some aspirin. I'm sure somebody must have. But I am not leaving this room until morning . . .

(I feel so empty. I have to keep thinking to use up the time. What would happen if I could stop thinking? Would I dissolve? I just sit here alone. How long has it been? It feels like hours. Maybe it is an hour. I am lonely, a little afraid. It goes on and on. And I am getting bored. What is the point? Why don't I stop? Why can't I just go to bed, or cry or anything? . . .

(When I was young I was much more hopeful. I seemed to expect things to be intense, even if they hurt. But now I have changed. I am growing afraid of being hurt. I would cross the street rather than see someone I didn't want to meet. I am an aging coward. Some vital part of the passage of everyday is slipping by me, like sand through fingers. There is something very wrong about that. The tide is running against me and I had not felt it. Why hadn't I felt it? Why hadn't I wanted myself to feel it? Oh, Marcia. Why don't you care anymore? Why do you watch the ships leaving without knowing whether they will return? If you don't care, who will?

(It is sad and you could cry about it. It is pathetic. You had it. And you are slowly losing it. There is nothing terribly wrong, just a few leaks that are growing larger, an accumulation of dust and decay that have not been taken care of.

(If that is what has happened, if that is why I cannot sleep, then I accept it. I don't want to sleep. I want to feel what I am and what I am becoming. Maybe then something different can emerge. But I don't really think so. I don't know how far down the roots go. I don't think I want to find out. I want to sleep. What is the use? It is all heading into the darkness.

(Somewhere out there two figures are watching. One says, "She will soon fall asleep and remember all this only as a late night fantasy or even a dream, interesting but unpleasant."

(The other says, "No. She is shaken. She will remember it in the sunshine. Even if she wishes to forget, the group will not permit it. They will not know what is happening unless she tells them, but they will unconsciously recognize the signs."

(Then they will be joined by a third person. That will be me in disguise, in a long white beard, and I will say, "A long time ago it was said that every clock runs down. She, being human and proud, had forgotten that fact. Now she is remembering. That is good."

(So they watch me and wonder what I will do, or if I will do anything, or if there is anything to do. I am getting so tired. But I can't lie down. Not yet. I must come to some decision.

(But is it possible? If I were a prize fighter I could decide that I needed to go into training because I had a match coming up. People are always able to take care of themselves if they are preparing for something destructive at the end. That is what I need. Something definite and continuous. But what? Where? I don't know what I am looking for.

(Suppose I was told that I had a rare disease, a gradual degeneration that need not be fatal if I undertook daily exercise to counteract its effects. Then I would be up and doing. But this way. There are so many demands and distractions. How can I ever work my way through them all? It seems like a crowded railroad station. All those people getting in the way.

(I want to lie down, go to sleep, and never wake up. It would really be nice to die quietly, or just to disappear. If only people wouldn't be upset. I do not want to face tomorrow. I really don't. I never wanted to be here in the first place. I can understand why people commit suicide. If it weren't for the fear of pain and damnation, who would want to see the whole thing through? For what?

(My mother used to say that it was too bad she had to sleep at night. It was such a waste of time. I thank God for sleep. It is a taste of death, an opportunity to withdraw. She was such a fool, though she meant so well. I wish that I had known it when she was alive. I could have loved her more and admired her less. Maybe that is part of the trouble. How could I ever plan anything without doing it her way, which wouldn't work for me? It didn't work for her. Mother, I am sorry for many things that I would say if you were here. But you are gone. So strange and so irrevocable. Except in a memory or dream. Perhaps you are with me now or out there drifting through the trees, drawn by your daughter's recollection of your life, which you yourself must almost have forgotten.

(I am really in a strange state. But I like it. Caught on the borderline of two worlds. What is real? Is the daylight real, food on the plate, going to the bathroom, getting dressed? Or is the nighttime real, with the sun down and the invisible stars emerging from the gloom, each a world with its own memories?

(I would like to sing to the stars a song about how their ancient light casts its memories upon me and holds me in a spell from which I do not wish to break. I want to go over to the bed with the starlight around me, slowly and gracefully; lie down quietly, keeping my motions like a seamless garment so that the spell is not broken. Letting my breath move gently in the twilight of its expectations, hearing the strange music which it brings to me, and the sense of expectation.

(I am so little. I am so frightened and dismayed by the sunlight. I am so alone, underneath the tiredness and behind the fear, lying here naked to the bone, stretched out a mirthless skeleton, having lost the allure of life, frightened of the outer space of death, looking for some guidance among creatures of the night, where it cannot be found, but still surrounded by the light of stars that protects me and draws me slowly, down, out, away, into a half-suspended state. My body here, my mind quiet, my emotions falling from me in a trembling husk, until my consciousness is taken from me in a sublime act of amnesia . . . )

# Saturday morning

General confusion; groans, stretching, and tension.

Richard: Did you get some sleep?

—What is sleep?

—Oh God, what a night!

Richard: We better do something to wake you all up in a hurry. Three times around the lodge.

Frank: Have a heart.

Richard: Everybody up and out.

Marcia: And for this we have to pay?

Richard: No talking. Later on you can tear me apart . . .

The room empties out under protest. Outside, the sounds of a herd of antelope, distant cries, screams, laughter, and then the group re-enters.

Richard: Did you have a good walk last night, Thurston?

Thurston: Is that any of your business?

Richard: Yes.

Thurston: I don't agree, not that anything so much happened. If I don't wish to share it with the group, I damn well won't.

Richard: While we are together, anything that happens must be open to all. If it is real it won't be destroyed. If it is not, it is better to find out even if it is painful.

Thurston: It is none of your business.

Richard: Why don't we reverse roles?

Thurston: I don't understand.

Richard: You be me and go on with the argument.

Thurston: All right. Maybe you'll learn something taking my part.

Thurston as Richard: So as I was saying, there is no such thing as privacy in an encounter group. We are all here to learn, not to have secrets from one another. Without access to information, how can we know what is happening?

Richard as Thurston: I can see your point, but I didn't make any such agreement when I signed up to come here. No one can make me tell the truth if I don't want to.

Thurston as Richard: I wouldn't want you to. But why do you fight it? Is it a matter of principle, or have you something to hide? The fact that you don't want to do it may prove that you should.

Richard as Thurston: That is the most immoral idea. If I go around being forced to do the things I don't want to do, I will do all kinds of horrible things.

Thurston as Richard: I doubt it. Usually the horrible things are what people want to do. They only lack the courage.

Richard as Thurston: You don't have a very optimistic view of human nature.

Thurston as Richard: I try to look at things as they are.

Richard: O.K., we are losing the thread. Anyway, Thurston, did you have a good walk last night?

Thurston: Yes, I did.

Richard: What was the most surprising part of it?

Thurston: I was most surprised that Penny wanted to come with me. She acted so much like a spoiled brat in the session. I didn't think she would want to associate with me. I wasn't very popular just then. But she did.

Richard: What part of the walk would you most like to tell us about?

Thurston: She seemed to like me. She said I reminded her of her father. He was a stuffed shirt too. I didn't mind it coming from her.

Richard: What part would you least like to tell us about?

Thurston: I really don't think it is necessary . . . Oh, we kissed, that was all. It wasn't funny.

Richard: I'm sure it wasn't.

Thurston: I thought Marcia was laughing at me.

Marcia: There I was up in my room unable to sleep and you were out having a great old time after telling us all that you were annoyed with us. It is funny, but it sounds nice.

Thurston: Are you satisfied? Has the group had its due?

Richard: Do you feel bad for having said it?

Thurston: I feel irritated with myself, like an embarrassed schoolboy. I hope I haven't offended Penny. I am married, you know. Nothing happened. Still I don't think my wife would understand how I came to be with some young girl kissing in the woods.

Penny: I am not "some girl."

Thurston: Why don't you stay out of this?

Penny: You are a big stiff goof. I kissed *you*, remember. All you did was respond a little bit. You weren't responsible.

Thurston: Who would believe you?

Richard: Are you really concerned about this?

Thurston: Well, I have heard some pretty wild stories about encounter groups. I have seen pictures in magazines about people in the nude and I have heard of marriages breaking up. My wife was nervous about my coming here.

Richard: So why are you here?

Thurston: She thought it might do me some good and I was somewhat curious.

Richard: Your wife thought that. Why?

Thurston: She wouldn't say. But she has been unhappy with me lately. I was never much of a lover.

Marcia: Are you saying that your wife wants you to be more romantic?

Thurston: I don't know. This is really a ridiculous situation. I am a perfectly happy man, better organized and directed than most. Not perfect, of course, but successful enough. I am sure the time could be better spent on someone else.

Richard: Perhaps. But here you are. What I would like to do is to ask the women in the group to react to you as they think your wife might. That may shed some light on what she had in mind sending you here.

Thurston: She didn't send me here. She encouraged me to come.

Richard: Why don't all the women form a small circle around Thurston and then express how they think Thurston's wife feels about him. Don't be polite. Say exactly what you think.

Thurston: I'm not sure I want to know. How can they possibly understand how my wife feels? They don't even know what she looks like.

Richard: Just shut up and listen!

—You are a good husband in many ways. Certainly you provide for us and I know that you aren't having any affairs. But you can be very stuffy.

—We haven't been dancing in years. I don't think you care for me. You don't even know I'm here half the time.

—I really don't like you. If I were free again I certainly wouldn't pick anyone like you. God, you are so boring.

Penny: I think you are sweet. If only you hadn't slowly died on me. But maybe that's unfair. Maybe you were always this way —reasonable, authoritative and dead. I just didn't want to see it.

I loved you and wanted the security of marriage. Now I know there are other things.

—Sometimes I just want to shake you. You are so sure you are right and everyone else is wrong.

Marcia: I just want you to be happier. You think you are happy but you don't know the meaning of the word. I don't want you to be different. Be as careful as you want. But let go a little. I don't want you to be irresponsible. But you could play a little more.

Silence.

Thurston: I don't think that is how she feels. I certainly hope to God it isn't.

Richard: What do you think her reasons were?

Thurston: Maybe it's her change of life. I don't think it has to do with me.

Richard: Do you really believe that, after what all these women have said?

Thurston: They are all part of this crazy atmosphere. They don't know me or her.

Richard: You know, I think you are absolutely right. I respect you for not letting yourself be influenced.

Thurston: Now what are you trying to pull?

Richard: I agree that your wife is probably projecting something onto you. I am glad that you are objective enough not to feel disturbed or guilty about it.

Thurston: Am I supposed to deny it because you agree with me? To hell with you.

Richard: Of course not. Just say what you think.

Thurston: I'm not perfect. But I try. That is more than a lot of people do. I don't agree with what you are doing, but I am willing to participate.

Richard: I respect you for that.

Thurston: I don't believe a word you say. I don't believe what anyone here says. I am beginning to think you planned all of this. Penny talked to you and then you arranged the whole thing.

Richard: Boy! That is remarkable. Most people wouldn't have figured it out.

Thurston: I am not most people.

Richard: Would you believe me if I said, "You are full of shit"?

Thurston: There is no need to be vulgar. I wouldn't believe anything you say.

Marcia: Do you believe anything I say?

Thurston: Nothing and nobody. I have had enough. Leave me alone. God damn it, leave me alone!

Richard: That is the first emotion I have heard you express, Thurston.

Thurston: Does it make you happy?

Richard: Yes. But is awfully hard work to get to it. You wear a very effective suit of armor.

Thurston: I want to. Would you have me walk around naked? You probably would.

Marcia: I got all wet leaning out of my window in the rain last night and then I stood in front of the mirror naked while I dried myself.

Thurston: Is that supposed to mean something? I am not a narcissist.

Frank: I'm sorry I wasn't there.

Richard: Maybe your wife doesn't like to be close to someone wearing a suit of armor. Maybe she wants you to be able to take it off when you get home at night. Let us ask the women again. Is it true? Does he go to bed with his armor on?

—The metal is cold.

—I know he didn't mean it, but I hurt myself on his spur.

—He creaks at night.

Thurston: I have had enough. Leave me alone.

Richard: What are you feeling, Thurston?

Thurston: You are trying to drive me up a tree.

Richard: Is any of this true?

Thurston: I don't know. How would I know? I just feel numb.

Richard: Lie down.

Thurston: What!

Richard: Don't give me a big argument. Lie down on the floor . . . That's right, with all the women around you. Now, Thurston . . . If you can, let some of the tension run out of your body and into the floor . . . That's right . . . Let the floor take over . . . and whenever they want to, I want the women to touch you . . . You just lie there and receive their touch, even if you don't think you want it. View it as an experiment.

(I put my hand on his forehead. It is cold and sweaty. He looks very old suddenly. Something has caved in. I wish he would breathe . . . that's better, but he is so pale . . . We have been hard on him . . . He is probably such a dutiful husband . . . so moral in a distant way . . . Probably giving very little and certainly taking very little from his wife . . . I feel sorry for her. But I am really sorry for him . . . I want to give him something . . . Maybe that is why Penny kissed him . . .

(He lies there, still tense, unable to experience what is happening . . . Why doesn't he just let go? I wish he could . . . Come on, Thurston . . . Are we that bad? . . . We have hurt you, but don't fight us off . . . There is nothing to fight. Melt . . . Melt . . . Melt . . . Breathe . . . That's better . . . I want to stroke his face. I wonder if that would be right? . . . If I want to, it must be all right . . .

(He probably thinks we are all after him . . . He is so suspicious . . . Poor baby. He would hate to be called that . . . Men are such children . . . So self-sufficient as long as someone is watching . . . His color is improving . . . It is sad. Probably what he needs most is to receive warmth . . . and here it is but he fights it off . . . And there is nothing to do but let it flow and hope that he will relax enough to begin to feel that it isn't so bad . . .

(It must be hard to be a man. There is so much you have to prove . . . I always felt a little cheated being a woman . . . But look at him . . . So much effort . . . so much energy just to keep things together . . . )

Richard: Now slowly remove your hands. Take your time. When they have all gone, lie there as long as you want. Let your sensations have a chance to settle, Thurston. Try to experience them, whatever they are. Don't force them and don't analyze them. Just observe and experience and most of all allow them to change . . . from one to another, to another . . .

There is no hurry . . . We are all here with you . . . We want you to take whatever time is necessary. We want you to have the chance to experience more of yourself . . . And when you are ready, open your eyes and gradually . . . sit up . . .

Thurston: . . . I feel upset.

Richard: Yes.

Thurston: I feel sad.

Richard: Yes.

Thurston: I feel happy too.

Richard: What is the first image that comes into your mind?

Thurston: A melting iceberg floating in the Gulf Stream.

Richard: Shut your eyes again and describe what you see . . . In fact, lie down . . . That's good . . . What does the iceberg look like? . . . What is happening to it?

Thurston: It is floating. It is dirty white on top . . . very cold and dark green underneath . . . There are a few birds on it . . . One of them is building a nest . . . It is hard to tell but it seems to be getting smaller . . . It must be melting . . . There is some smoke on the horizon . . . but no ship . . .

Richard: Where are you?

Thurston: Watching. Now I am coming closer . . . The iceberg feels like melting slush. I thought it was more solid. The water is quite warm. It has some kind of small organisms in it. They are green and slimy. They are covering the bottom like a grass stain. Oh . . . a part of the iceberg just broke off and is floating away . . . getting smaller . . . but I am on the big chunk . . . now another small part is breaking up . . . it is dissolving . . . Where am I going to stand? . . . The bird building the nest is looking around. It has a yellow marking on its forehead, almost golden . . . It is going to fly away . . .

Silence.

Richard: What is happening?

Thurston: It has gone. The whole picture is receding. I must be seeing it like the bird . . . getting higher, . . . circling around . . . the ocean far below . . . I am fogged in a cloud. I am riding on the bird. I feel very free. I hope I don't fall off . . .

Richard: Open your eyes.

Thurston: What happened?

Richard: Do you feel different?

Thurston: I don't know about that, but you all look very different. You all seem so concerned. I forgot that you were here . . . Thank you.

Frank: For what?

Thurston: For having the interest and the patience . . .

Richard: There may be some people here who want to express something to you. Would you be willing to hear them?

Thurston: Yes, if they really want to . . .

Marcia: You looked so old and helpless when you were lying there at first, almost afraid to breathe. I wanted you to breathe, but there was nothing I could do but hope . . .

Thurston: I don't know what to say. It was a rather terrifying experience.

Marcia: Why?

Penny: I thought you said you were physically weak.
Ann: How would you like to wrestle?
Penny: Are you kidding?
Ann: Don't you want to? I won't tickle.
Richard: Do you have anything against Penny?
Ann: I just feel like wrestling. How about it?
Penny: Somebody hold my glasses and my watch.

They stand about five feet apart, looking one another over, coming closer. Suddenly Ann moves forward, grabbing Penny around the waist and pulling her down . . . They roll around on the floor . . . Penny tries to get Ann off her, but Ann is playing to win . . . She almost has Penny pinned when Penny breaks away, stands up and moves to the side of the room.

Penny: Is that enough?
Ann: I don't care. It's enough for me.
Richard: Before you retire, why don't you two sit in the center of the room and talk with each other about what just happened.
Ann: I don't have anything to say.
Penny: I do. So sit . . . When was the last time you wrestled with a woman, or with anybody?
Ann: With a woman, a long time ago, with my younger sister. I must have been eleven. We used to have some great fights.
Penny: Did you like her?
Ann: Well, she was a pain in the ass but I liked her. I was lonely when she wasn't around.
Penny: I don't think I ever wrestled with a woman in my whole life. I was scared of you.
Ann: Of me? Why? I didn't want to hurt you.
Penny: I realized that when we started. But I didn't know what you picked on me for. I've wrestled with men. But with women it's different.
Richard: Did you think she might be a Lesbian?

Penny: It had crossed my mind. If a woman wants to get very physical with me, what am I supposed to think?

Ann: What do you think!

Penny: Listen, it was a new experience for me. I wanted to get away from you, but I enjoyed it.

Ann: I enjoyed it too.

Richard: We can't help thinking along these lines, but we don't have to accept it. We are people, many different people. We are grownup and we are children. As the child emerges, the grownup can confuse innocence with circulation. We usually think of ourselves as tolerant and accepting of others. It isn't so. We tear other people apart, label them, ridicule them, and fear them with a rapidity and aplomb that is astonishing. The only thing that is uncomfortable is confessing it in public. If we keep these things to ourselves or to our own group, and never let the person concerned know what we think, it is all right. It is easy. Unfortunately for the other person, the one thing we don't want to say is likely to be the thing he needs most to know.

Penny: How do you feel about me now?

Ann: At first you reminded me of my sister. But now that is gone. You are more fragile than I thought. Your sarcasm is a front. I feel quite comfortable with you, somewhat attracted by you. But if I were a man I would find you a little insipid.

Richard: While you two are sitting there talking to one another, does anyone watching have any impressions? Are you interested in what is going on? If you are bored, say so.

Silence.

Richard: In that case, I am going to suggest that we have a short group fantasy about Penny and Ann. Everybody shut his eyes, visualize the two of them sitting there, and then, in your imagination, allow whatever you want to happen. When you see something say it out loud. Ann and Penny, I want you to act out the fantasy as it is described. You are actors performing to someone else's script. You do what you are told. You have no responsibility for it.

Penny: Suppose I don't want to?

Richard: You are a puppet. You have no initiative. If you find anything embarrassing or offensive, you can express it somewhat symbolically. But represent everything that is said. Everyone shut his eyes and begin.

Pause.

Frank: They are just sitting there looking at one another intently. Now there is a fog between them. The images blur. Then the fog disperses and they have become a snake and a monkey. Ann is the snake. The monkey stares, fascinated, unable to move. The snake moves gracefully, never taking its gaze from the monkey. Now the snake begins to curl around the monkey. It is going to squeeze the monkey.

Ann has grasped Penny around her waist and begins to tighten. Penny struggles to breathe.

Marcia: The monkey lets out all its breath. It seems to shrink. It escapes from the snake. It is running up a tree.

Penny climbs on a chair.

Marcia: It swings away from the snake.

She jumps to a chest.

Thurston: That is not what I see. There are two little girls, each in party dresses and sucking big lollipops. They stick out their tongues at each other . . . They put their thumbs in their ears and waggle their fingers. They smear one another with their lollipops . . . Now they start to hit at one another as if they were fencing. What a mess . . . They start to lick their arms to get off the stickiness . . .

Frank: I see them changing into two young men. They look at each other, surprised, smiling. They touch. They are women who look like men. Their feelings are mixed up. As women they are attracted to men. As men they are guarded. They hug each other but act embarrassed. They begin to arm wrestle . . . but seem to feel silly . . . Then a beautiful girl walks past. They get up and follow her, but are uncertain about what they will do, or how to approach her. As they get up they change back into women.

Richard: That's enough. Open your eyes. And look at them.

Ann: That was a weird experience.

Richard: In what way?

Ann: I felt so free even though I had no freedom. I could have done almost anything as long as it was someone else's idea.

Richard: And you, Penny?

Penny: I feel exhilarated, but I am scared. I am stirred up. There are so many things I might do if I were willing to allow myself. Where will it stop?

Richard: It hasn't really started.

Penny: You can say that. You weren't in the experience. How do I know I will be able to control myself? Maybe I will do something I could regret later on.

Richard: Such as?

Penny: I don't know, hurt somebody or get involved sexually.

Richard: Love and death, sex and aggression.

Penny: You are inhuman.

Richard: It doesn't matter what I am. The only thing that you have to worry about is what it does for you. If I hurt you for no reason, or drive you farther than you should go, that is bad. If I hide my real motives, that is bad. If I use my power in this situation to seduce women, etc., that is bad. I am not saying that I am above having a personal relationship with any one of you, but I can't do it undercover. But what about your experience did you react to especially?

Ann: It was interesting being a snake. I knew Penny was scared of me and that made it more enjoyable.

Penny: You are a bloodthirsty creature.

Ann: "I was only following orders," as the storm trooper said. I was hoping I might get to crush you to death.

Penny: Are you serious?

Ann: Haven't you ever wanted to become as tight as you could and just crush and crush?

Penny: You really are a monster.

Ann: You never have? Not an insect, not in a dream. I don't believe it.

Penny: Are you for real?

Ann: Right now I am very real. I don't care what you think. I don't care what anybody thinks. You can all go fuck yourselves! You too, Richard.

Richard: That's the nicest thing you have said to me.

Penny: Is this the kind of expression you want, Richard?

Richard: What do you think?

Penny: I thought I knew, but I am being shaken. I thought this was a good experience, but there is something horrifying about it.

Richard: We are all held in bondage. Society does not trust us and we do not trust ourselves. We are painfully and carefully socialized. If the bonds are loosened, what emerges is not necessarily pleasant. Everything Ann is expressing, you have inside yourself. If you could experience and accept it, you would not be horrified.

Penny: I don't want to experience it. Life is cruel enough without my being brought down to its level.

Richard: What do you mean?

Penny: People hate each other. I know what goes on.

Richard: There are two countries. In one there is life. People feel, act, and experience. In the other there is death. People are anesthetized. You must choose. It is easier to be half asleep. But if you choose the first, then you must experience all of it.

Penny: I don't trust you.

Richard: Did you ever?

Penny: Perhaps not.

Richard: You never will as you are. If you can't experience that within you which is capable of evil, then you are at its mercy. I am not trying to create monsters, but you have to accept that monsters live within you . . .

Thurston: I remember wanting to kill my father.

Frank: Did you say something?

Thurston: Yes. I said, "I remember wanting to kill my father."

Richard: Instead of telling us about it, could you act it out?

Thurston: I don't mind.

Richard: Could Frank be your father?

Thurston: Yes.

Richard: What is the situation?

Thurston: It was very simple. My father got drunk and was beating up my mother and I wanted to kill him.

Richard: Not so fast. Pick someone to be your mother.

Thurston: It doesn't matter. How about Penny?

Richard: Are you willing?

Penny: If it will help, but I don't really want to.

Richard: Did this happen often or just once?

Thurston: More than once. But I am thinking of one time in particular.

Richard: You seem very calm about the whole thing.

Thurston: It is only a memory.

Richard: Can you describe the setting?

Thurston: We were living in a suburb of Cleveland. I was about thirteen and I woke up when they started shouting.

Richard: Are you in bed?

Thurston: I was asleep. I thought I was dreaming and then . . .

Richard: Lie down. Do it just as it was. You are asleep. Which side do you sleep on?

Thurston: How should I know? The left, I guess. And suddenly I wake up and . . .

Richard: Stop! What is the first thing you feel?

Thurston: I am startled. My heart is beating fast. I think I must have had a nightmare. But the voices are continuing. They are shrieking. He is laughing that harsh horrible laugh and cursing at her.

Richard: Go ahead, curse her.

Frank as Father: You God damn whore! I'll teach you to talk back to me.

Richard: Is that right?

Thurston: She cries at him to keep away or she will hit him with a bottle.

Penny as Mother: You drunken bum. Stay away or I'll give it to you between the eyes.

Thurston: I get up then and walk to the door in my pajamas.

Richard: What is the first thing you see?

Thurston: He has gotten the bottle away from her and he hits her hard across the face. I can still see the whole side of her face getting red and beginning to swell up. And I want to stop him. I want to hurt him. I want him to die.

Richard: What do you do?

Thurston: I stand there. He moves away. He doesn't see me. My mother looks stunned. They both must have been drunk. They don't see me. They never knew I was there. They still don't.

Richard: You never talked to your mother about it?

Thurston: Never! I was too scared, but I sometimes asked her about my father. I never got anywhere though.

Richard: Try now. Where would you talk to her?

Thurston: In the kitchen.

Richard: Then arrange the furniture and begin.

Penny: Shouldn't I know something more?

Richard: Go ahead.

Thurston: I couldn't sleep well last night.

Penny as Mother: Your father and I were arguing.

Thurston: Why do you fight so much?

Mother: When you get older you will understand better.

Thurston: I am old enough now. I hate him for what he does to you.

Mother: What does he do to me?

Thurston: Why do you stay with him? You don't need him.

Mother: There are things that are hard to understand. He needs me. He may not act it.

Richard: Is this how it goes?

Thurston: Not exactly, but I don't get anywhere. That is the same.

Richard: How does it end?

Thurston: Oh, she gives me some milk and cookies and I am disgusted with her and myself.

Richard: Would you like to have another chance to talk with her?

Thurston: It wouldn't make any difference.

Richard: How can you know? I am offering you a chance to fulfill something that was left undone. Don't throw it away.

Thurston: All right. I finish the milk and cookies. And I say, "I was awake last night."

Mother: What!

Thurston: And I came into the room and saw him hit you!

Mother: I didn't see you.

Thurston: You were too drunk to see me. It was really bad. I wanted to hit him. I wanted to hurt him.

Mother: You don't understand.

Thurston: Why not? He is an animal. He should be in jail. Why don't you have him put away?

Mother: You are awfully anxious to get rid of your father.

Thurston: Some people shouldn't be allowed to live.

Mother: What!

Thurston: I wish he were dead.

Mother: He may be a bastard, but I certainly don't want him dead. He has been getting worse. I didn't know it affected you so much. Maybe I will leave him. Maybe not. But you mustn't think such things. He is your father, the only one you have. You should respect him.

Thurston: Do you?

Mother: When he is angry, I sure do, sonny.

Richard: Is there anything else you want to say to your mother?

Thurston: If you want me to protect you, I will!

Mother: My little knight. What could you do? I can take care of myself all right, sweetheart.

Richard: You don't really look happy, Thurston. You haven't gotten rid of it yet.

Thurston: She was a stupid woman. She must have enjoyed it. Maybe it proved to her that he loved her. But I still hate him.

Richard: What finally happened?

Thurston: He left her. I don't know whether he is alive or dead.

Richard: I want to try one more thing, Thurston. I want you to go over to the couch at the end of the room. Everyone get off it and give him room . . . Now kneel down and start pounding the cushions . . . Do it slowly and let it build up.

Clouds of dust come out as Thurston hits the pillows.

Richard: Don't stop . . . As you hit, start cursing . . . Really mean it . . .

Thurston: You . . . God . . . damn . . . son of a bitch . . . You lousy . . . motherfucker . . . you cruel bastard . . . I hate you . . . I want to beat you to a pulp . . . I want to see your blood on the floor . . . I want . . .

Richard: Start to make noises as you hit . . . Grunt, scream . . . anything.

Thurston keeps hitting and hitting. He grunts. Then he begins wild shouting, and screaming—angry, murderous, piercing. Suddenly he folds up and begins to sob in tight convulsions.

Richard: Let it go. Let it all come out.

Thurston: I don't want . . . to cry . . . I hate him. Why should I cry for him? . . . I don't . . . want . . . to give . . . him the . . . satisfaction.

Richard: Let it come. Don't stop now.

Thurston: Oh, God. I don't want this. I don't want to feel this. I feel awful. I want to die. I want to forget. What is happening? I must be going out of my mind.

Richard: Talk to your father. If he were here, what would you say to him?

Thurston: I want to kill him and I want him to forgive me.

Richard: Talk to him. Don't explain what you would do.

Thurston: Isn't there any end? Don't you have mercy? . . . Father, Father, I can't escape you. I thought it was all over. I am grown-up. You are gone. But I can't forget you and what you did. I can't forget how I feel about you. If you were here, I would choke you. Can you understand? Why did you desert us? Why did you go away? What did I do to you? It was never the same after you left . . . never ever the same again . . . I have tried to find my way. I have done what I thought was right . . . I have tried, but I don't know where to go now. I don't know what to do. I can't escape you. Help me to get away.

Richard: Do you have any idea where your father is?

Thurston: No.

Richard: Become your father and talk to your son, Thurston.

Thurston: I can't.

Richard: Try.

Thurston as Father: So you have grown to be a man, have

you? . . . You still think about me sometimes, do you? . . . I
am old now . . . weak, sick . . . I am dying. I think of you
sometimes, wondering if I should try to see you before I die.
But you wouldn't want to have anything to do with me. I'll let
the past alone. I'm sorry if I hurt you, Thurston. You were a
funny kid. I didn't know you were there most of the time. You
don't understand. How could you understand when you never
had a good drunk in your whole life.

Richard: Do you understand?

Thurston: I am feeling very chilly. I want a blanket.

Marcia: Here, Thurston. Wrap this around you.

Thurston: Thank you. That is very good of you. I am not myself. I feel like I am coming down with a fever. I don't know
what I am saying.

Richard: Yes, yes, yes. You have earned a rest. Be sick for a
while. Be a little boy in bed, home from school, being taken care
of by his mother.

Thurston lies down on the couch, puts his blanket around him,
shuts his eyes and shivers from time to time.

Frank: What happens now?

Marcia: Wasn't that enough?

Frank: I feel stupid and helpless.

Richard: The natural thing is to go numb. The way to avoid it
is to keep the experience flowing. What did it do to any of you?
What did it bring up in your own experience?

Ann: Isn't there any end?

Richard: There are a number of people who have remained
in the background. I wish they would say something about what
the experience meant to them.

—I don't know why I haven't said anything. My name is John.
I find it hard to express what I feel.

Richard: Do you feel anything? Does the situation remind
you of anything in your own experience?

John: I don't think that I have ever seen my parents fight. But what I would most like to do right now is run through the woods as fast as I could until I was so tired I would collapse on the ground.

Richard: Have you ever done that?

John: In college. I was a long-distance runner. If I kept going long enough my whole perspective changed. The only real thing was the running. Everything else was background. I felt safe then and powerful. I was in my own world. Now I feel vulnerable, waiting for the searchlight to swing in my direction.

Richard: What do you do when you can't run?

John: I keep my mouth shut. But you won't let me do that any more.

Richard: I don't think you want to or you wouldn't have spoken up. There are other silent people here. Why don't you start running around the room and continuing talking.

John: That would be silly.

Richard: How about imagining yourself running through the woods? Can you do that and continue to talk at the same time?

John: That I like! O.K., I am in the woods running and I am here sitting. Why didn't I ever think of that? That's a brilliant idea. I am here and not here. I am much safer. Out there you cannot stop me. I simply run faster. There is a path winding through the woods. I am free of all of you.

Richard: What about yourself?

John: Myself most of all.

Richard: Tell us about an experience you have had that Thurston has reminded you of.

John: I can do that. I remember beating up a girl once. I don't feel so good about that.

Richard: How well did you know her?

John: We were engaged. I caught her making out with someone else. I didn't actually catch her, but I found out about it. I was about nineteen. And I just said, "You bitch" and I slapped her hard in the face. She just walked off. Not a word. Not a tear. I guess she knew she deserved it. I really enjoyed that moment. Afterward I began to feel bad though. I called her up and asked her to forgive me. That was a big mistake. She said if I ever came near her she would call the police. I never saw her again.

Richard: Did you fall in love again?

John: I am in love now, I guess.

Richard: Is she faithful?

John: You mean would I hit her if she weren't? I don't know. It's not the same. I feel more comfortable with Caroline. She isn't always stringing me along with feminine psychology, acting helpless and cute.

Richard: How is the running coming along?

John: Just fine. While I am at it, I just remembered once when I was with my father. We were fishing and he spent a long time getting the line straightened out and I wanted to cast it. He told me not to, but I did it anyway. It got all tangled in the trees. He hit me then and I was very angry. I can turn white when I get angry. But it passed. Adults don't realize how unfair it is to hit kids. They are so defenseless.

Richard: Why are you running, John?

John: I told you why. I feel free. I can escape from myself.

Richard: Why don't you fly in the air?

John: Because I can't.

Richard: You could in your mind.

John: But I know that I can't. I can run though. And you can't catch me.

Richard: But if we did catch you, what then?

John: Then something bad would happen. You would rob me or take something precious from me. That sounds crazy, doesn't it?

Richard: Maybe not. Start running.

John: I already am.

Richard: Not just in your mind. Start running around the room where we can catch you. Stay in the room though.

John begins to move around slowly at first, and then setting a regular rhythm.

Richard: Everybody up. We are going to catch him. When you do, just act any way you want to.

The group spreads out, half-heartedly at first. They do not really want to catch John. He certainly doesn't want to be caught. He eludes them on the ground. Then he takes to furniture. Finally he pushes them away until four or five of the group converge on him and pull him down struggling. They relax and he escapes . . . They go after him. This time they do not relax. He struggles harder. The odds are too great.

John: Let me go! I won't run any more. Just let me go, I can't stand to be held.

Richard: Let him go. What's the trouble?

John: When people are too close to me, I get panicky. I hate subways.

Richard: What did you think was going to happen to you?

John: It was a horrible feeling of being held down, choked, throttled. It was like being at the bottom of a pile-up on a football field. Only they don't get up. I have to throw them off. And I can't. I just can't. There are too many of them.

I can't seem to get my breath. No matter how deeply I breathe, I am stifled. There isn't enough oxygen.

Richard: Can you feel your heart beating?

John: Yes, it is going very fast.

Richard: Concentrate on the beating. Feel it spreading out through you. Put all your attention on that . . . Do you feel better?

John: Yes. That helps. I really was getting scared, but I

don't know of what exactly. If I could remember some incident.

Richard: Then what?

John: That might explain it.

Richard: Don't get hung-up on the past. Maybe there was a
specific thing. Maybe only fantasies. Maybe the whole situation
is symbolic and never happened in any form. The point is that
you are running in the present because you don't want to get
held down and smothered. Who does? It is natural. The thing
that is bad is that you don't trust yourself enough to be able to
survive the reactions of other people. If your own sense of yourself were stronger, you could walk. You could even sit quietly
and no one could really touch you. But at least there must be
something inside you that you want to protect. You should be
thankful for that.

John: There really is. I don't know how to describe it. Perhaps
it is a small candle that is burning. It doesn't seem like much,
but I know that as long as it burns I am all right. If it goes out,
I am dead, even though it might take five years for the effects
to be visible on the surface. Sometimes I feel like a relay runner
carrying a torch that has to be handed on to someone else whom
I have never met.

Richard: Where did you get it?

John: I was running and someone put it in my hand.

Richard: You didn't have to take it.

John: No, but I did take it. I wanted to, but I didn't realize
what it would involve, that I could never stop running until
someone appeared to take it from me.

Richard: Could you give it to anyone here?

John: I don't dare. I might be wrong. It is not for me to decide.
I don't really like to talk about it. It must sound crazy.

Marcia: I think it is beautiful.

John: It is more like a curse. Who needs it?

Marcia: It is probably the most important thing about you. I really feel that you are a character out of Greek mythology. It makes me feel different talking to you. We might be in some hidden grove on a sunlit island. You are resting, safe for a brief time. I wash you off, undo your shoes and bathe your feet in oil. You do not trust me right away. Slowly you relax.

John: It sounds very good. But I don't feel like a hero—more like a coward who cannot avoid his fate.

Marcia: That is a modern hero.

Richard: It is nearly lunch time. Everyone must be shell-shocked. I want to suggest that after lunch we meet in groups of two. Go together wherever you want to go and share with each other as directly and honestly as you can. Would you pick someone and arrange where you will meet? We will come back together here at 3:00 . . .

# Saturday afternoon

Marcia: The air smells of smoke. Must be from the kitchen. Shall we follow the path or just take off into the forest?

John: Let's follow the path and see where it goes . . .

Marcia: Why did you pick me?

John: I thought you picked me . . . We are supposed to be frank. So tell me what you think of me.

Marcia: Haven't you had enough this morning?

John: That was this morning. This is now.

Marcia: Suppose we go over there under that old pine tree and sit down.

John: I would rather walk.

Marcia: It won't kill you to sit. No, you sit there and I will rest against the tree and I will tell you what I think of you . . .

John: I am waiting.

Marcia: I am thinking. This whole situation is a little crazy.

John: So tell me.

Marcia: Why don't you tell me what you think of me? Do you like me?

John: I hardly know you.

Marcia: I hardly know you.

John: Well, we have something in common.

Marcia: This is real stupid, like conversations on a first date.

What is supposed to happen anyway? How are things going to be different here than they ever were anywhere else?

John: How about climbing a tree?

Marcia: Go ahead.

John: All right.

He reaches up to the first branch of the tree Marcia is resting against, pulls himself up and starts climbing. As he goes he knocks down pine needles and little branches. Marcia lies back on the ground to watch him go.

Marcia: You look like a skinny bear.

John: What?

Marcia: You look like a SKINNY BEAR!

John: Oh! I'm going to go almost to the top. I can't even see you any more.

Marcia: What is it like up there?

John: I can't tell until I get to the top. If you hear a big crash, get out of the way in a hurry . . . Hey, there are lots of birds here suddenly. They seemed surprised to see me . . . O.K. I am as high as I can go. I can see over the trees. The sun is shining. If I wasn't scared I would try to fly.

Marcia: Leave that for the birds.

John: There is a stream about one hundred yards away. There are farms in the distance. There are even storm clouds, but the wind is blowing the other way . . . I am going to stay here a minute, then I'm coming down.

(I wish I had tried to climb. But it is too late now . . . What do I like about him? He is elusive. He likes to move through space. I don't really know anything specific about him, just a vague impression . . .)

John: Get up! We are going to the stream.

Marcia: Which way?

John: Just follow me. Let's run . . .

They take off into the forest . . .

Marcia: (*panting*) That was . . . fun . . . but . . . I got all scratched up.

John: Bathe with some cool water. Here, let me.

Marcia: Oh. That feels good . . . Do you plan to get undressed?

John: No, just my shoes, socks, and shirt. I want to feel the water. How would you like it if I got my shirt soaked and then squeezed it out over your hair?

Marcia: Don't you dare!

John: I think that would be a great idea . . . Don't run. You know I can catch you. Just enjoy it!

Marcia: Oh my God, it is freezing.

John: Here, you do it to me.

Marcia: With pleasure.

John: I didn't say to hit me. Just gently wring it out.

Marcia: I didn't say to wring it out. Just shut up and enjoy it.

John: How would you like me to throw you in the water?

Marcia: The last time I was thrown in the water was when I was eight years old. I didn't like it then and I wouldn't like it now.

John: You want to throw me in?

Marcia: I couldn't.

John: You really don't want me to throw you in?

Marcia: Are you out of your mind? It is freezing.

John: You didn't answer the question.

Marcia: Aren't we supposed to talk to one another or something?

John: To hell with that . . . IN YOU GO . . . (*laughing his head off*) You look like an oversized doused wet rabbit.

Marcia: (*teeth chattering*) I . . . am . . . not–t–t amused. What kind of a maniac are you anyway?

John: You must admit you feel more awake.

Marcia: I feel like I am going to come down with pneumonia.

John: Lie down on the grass. I will warm you up.

Marcia: Just what do you have in mind?

John: Come on. I'll give you a massage.

Marcia: I think you have done enough. I want to go back.

John: Don't be so up-tight. I am not going to rape you. And the longer you argue, the colder you will get. Lie down. If you don't feel better in five minutes we can go back.

Marcia: We can go back right now, if I decide to, but go ahead. I am freezing.

Marcia lies down on her stomach. John straddles her and begins slapping her back.

Marcia: That is a rubdown?

John: I am warming you up. Is it too hard?

Marcia: No, I would rather hurt than freeze.

He leans forward and starts to tap with his fingers on her neck and the back and sides of her head.

John: If you want to make some kind of sound, go ahead.

Marcia: Like what—"Goo goo?"

John: Whatever you like—loud, soft, tones, noises.

Marcia: I used to go ah–ah–ah when my father would hit my back. Ah–ah–ah . . .

John: You have a nice body.

Marcia: Thank you. My legs are cold.

He shifts down and slaps the back of her legs.

Marcia: Easy. That hurts!

John: If it doesn't hurt, you won't get warm. Think of how great it will feel when I stop . . . There. Turn over.

Marcia: Can I trust you?

John: To do what? Don't be so suspicious.

For five minutes they are quiet. John works on her legs, stomach, shoulders, neck, head; slapping, patting, and rubbing. Marcia withdraws into herself and relaxes.

John: O.K. Get up! We are going for a fast walk!

Marcia: I want to lie here.

John: If you don't get up, you will just get cold again. We can walk and talk . . .

Marcia: The air really smells wonderful now. Thank you.

John: You weren't so thankful before.

Marcia: I was wrong. I guess I am a physical coward.

John: How do you feel about me now?

Marcia: That's where it all began. I feel different things. You are very unpredictable. But I think that I trust you. I don't mean that naively. I am sure there are things in you that would bother me, but all in all, I do.

John: How about while I was working on you?

Marcia: I wanted to give myself up to the sensation, but I didn't quite dare, at first. I would have been too much at your mercy. Weren't you tempted?

John: To do what?

Marcia: To make love to me.

John: Is that what you wanted?

Marcia: I'm asking the questions.

John: If you mean do I find you attractive, the answer is yes. But I think women have the idea that men automatically want to have intercourse whenever the possibility exists.

Marcia: Don't they?

John: No.

Marcia: This is a pretty crazy conversation.

John: No, it isn't. You want to know whether you can get warm without being burned. It doesn't matter what I say. You have to find out for yourself. Sometimes when I look at a woman I want to leave the room. Sometimes I feel aroused, sometimes just warm.

Marcia: How do you feel when you look at me?

John: I don't think you really want to know. You are being coy. I don't want to play games with you.

Marcia: Sometimes I wish I didn't have a body. It makes so many demands. It gets in the way. People see it. They don't see me. Men are attracted to it. I don't mean that I don't enjoy attracting. If I didn't I would feel bad, but it is all an illusion. Would you be attracted by what is inside? Would we be together if it weren't for sex?

John: I don't know. In my better moments sex is a fire. It warms me, wakes me up; but it can also abuse me. What nature wants from me and what I want from nature are two different things. Sometimes intercourse can be a great climax. But it often seems to me that the earlier stages are the most satisfying. They are much more mysterious and promising.

Marcia: I don't think I have ever talked with a man about sex. I have always been too involved in the situation, keeping him off or encouraging him. It is so hard to be friends with a man. There are so many innuendoes.

John: Why don't you pretend that we are masked strangers? We don't know who the other is and we will never meet again. You are free to ask anything you want of me as a man. I don't mean actions, but any questions?

Marcia: I feel embarrassed . . . I suppose what I would like to know is what it feels like being a man.

John: You mean having a penis?

Marcia: I suppose so. But that sounds awfully crude.

John: Most of the time I don't even know it's there. If it's any comfort to you, I feel embarrassed too. I suppose these things could be discussed clinically, like doctors or physiologists describing an interesting process. But that would be horrible. What I said before about the early stages sometimes being the best. The first moment an erection starts can feel wonderful. Later I may get over-stimulated. That can be uncomfortable or just urgent.

There is a fantasy I used to have. I wanted to make love

with someone very slowly and describe just what I was feeling as it happened. It sounds cold-blooded but I have always felt it could be tremendous.

Marcia: I don't understand.

John: Say I just looked at you, as I am doing now. What does that do to you? Can you describe your sensation?

Marcia: My cheeks feel warmer. It spreads down into my throat. I want to swallow.

John: Now if I put my hand on your throat, how does that feel?

Marcia: Scary. My heart is beating faster. I am breathing deeper.

John: Now I am going to kiss you for a few seconds . . . How was that?

Marcia: It went right down through me. That doesn't usually happen. I must feel very relaxed.

John: Well, that is the idea. Except we would have to go into areas and sensations that usually aren't shared. I would tell you and you would tell me. Each action would lead on to the next. That is my daydream.

Marcia: Why are you stopping? You haven't had a chance to respond to me.

John: First I better calm down for a minute.

Marcia: That sounds interesting.

John: No, it is only confusing. Do you really want to know or just satisfy your womanly pride?

Marcia: What should I do first?

John: That is up to you.

Marcia: Then I will just stand here about a foot away.

John: I am very aware of you there. I feel warmth in my solar plexus. You seem like a dish waiting to be tasted. I am slightly aroused, a tingling, a warmth. I would like to . . .

Marcia: To what?

John: To put my hands on your breasts.

Marcia: Fortunately you can't. I am the one making the moves. Now I am going to put my hand on the back of your neck.

John: It feels very warm . . . friendly . . . but quiet. The warmth goes into my head and down my spine. It is soothing.

Marcia: Do you still want to put your hands there?

John: Not so much, but I could force myself.

Marcia: Now I am going to turn my back and stand right in front of you, barely touching.

John: That sends me off sexually. I have an erection now. My penis is throbbing.

Marcia: Very interesting. The experiment is over.

John: Do you enjoy making me uncomfortable?

Marcia: I enjoy making you want me.

John: Suppose I stop playing the game.

Marcia: You wouldn't, would you?

John: No. I might throw you in the water, but I am not going to attack you.

Marcia: We are playing with fire.

John: Yes. I can feel it burning between us.

Marcia: It is warming me from below.

John: Nature wants intercourse and children. That is the simplest and crudest use of sex. But the force itself is very subtle and extraordinarily intense, if people could learn to experience it without being swept away.

Marcia: You are a very strange person. I don't know very much more about you than I did before. And you know nothing about me and my life. You don't know if I am married, divorced, engaged, in love. But it doesn't seem to matter.

John: No, it doesn't.

Marcia: I feel very good. My clothes are still wet, but I am warm. There are tears in my eyes. I am very emotional. Why? I am making a fool of myself.

John: Put your warm face and wet shirt next to me and cry if you want to.

Marcia: I do.

He holds her and she sobs quietly.

Marcia: I don't know why I should be so sad. I was up half the night. It's this place. These people.

John: You don't have to explain yourself. Just cry.

Marcia: It feels like raindrops coming out of my eyes. I want to lie down and let my teardrops fall on the earth.

John: The earth can absorb everything, all the poisons, all the regrets, all the longing.

Marcia: I could really learn to hate you.

John: Good, let that out too.

Marcia: I don't want to be naked. I don't want people to know what I am.

John: Good.

Marcia: It's not good. It's terrible. Stop being so God damn agreeable. Stop making me want to love you.

John: Don't get too warm. You may scare me away.

Marcia: Would I? I don't think so. Would you climb another tree? You would still have to come down again. How can I feel so much for someone I just met?

John: You don't know me. It must be an illusion.

Marcia: You know damn well it isn't. Why must you be so irritating?

John: Some people are just talented.

Marcia: And stop being so defensive.

John: You know me, the long-distance fantasy runner.

Marcia: I don't care what you say or what you do. It isn't going to turn me away.

John: That is what you say now.

Marcia: You must have been burned.

John: Haven't you been?

Marcia: That's different.

John: Sure it's different. It happened to you. I have had all I can take right now. Let's go back to the group . . .

*Saturday, midafternoon*

Penny: So you two finally decided to return.

Marcia: What time is it?

Penny: 3:30.

Marcia: I have to change my clothes.

Ann: You look as if you fell into a stream.

Marcia: Thrown was more like it. I'm going to change . . .

Richard: Why don't you stay now that you are here? Does anybody want to say anything about their "diads"?

Frank: Their what?

Richard: "Diads"—two-person groups.

Frank: Do we have to?

Richard: How can I make you if you don't want to?

Frank: That is no answer. You are very evasive sometimes. In fact I have yet to see anyone pin you down about anything.

Richard: Would you like to try?

Frank: I just want to feel free to say you have a few weaknesses too.

Ann: What were you doing this afternoon?

Richard: What do you think?

Ann: If I knew I wouldn't ask. Hey Frank, I see what you mean.

Richard: What do you imagine I was doing?

Ann: I honest to God don't know. Were you sleeping?

Richard: No.

Ann: Were you with someone?

Richard: Yes. Can you guess who?

Ann: Was it a woman?

Richard: Do you think it was?

Ann: Yes.

Richard: It wasn't. I was with Thurston.

Ann: Oh. I guess that ends that conversation.

Richard: You're not curious about what happened?

Ann: No. I figure he was still upset and you were talking to him. By the way, what happens when you get upset? You do get upset sometimes, don't you? Suppose you blow your cork, where does that leave us?

Richard: Let's hope we don't have to find out. Is there anyone else with bad feelings about me?

John: I don't have bad feelings. You are certainly good at stirring things up and keeping them going, but I wonder whether you could control them if they began to get out of hand.

Richard: What do you think might happen?

John: You are opening up a lot of dark closets. Part of it is wonderful and exhilarating. But the tension is getting pretty great. I don't know what is going to happen next. Do you?

Richard: No, I don't. Usually what I expect to happen is what doesn't happen. If I try and force it, the results are bad.

Thurston: I don't much feel like talking but I feel less responsible for what I do. That frightens me. I am in a bad dream in which all sorts of strange, wild and possibly terrible things happen. You wake up from a dream and leave it behind. But can we wake up from this?

Richard: Are you all trying to find out whether or not I am frightened? Sometimes I am. But the greater the tension, the more I tend to sink down into myself. Perhaps that is the trouble right now. You are scared of the emotions and energies inside yourself because you don't have any strong sense of yourself. You lack a center of gravity.

Do you want to try an experiment? . . . Sit down in

a circle. Keep your eyes open at first. Later when we begin you can shut them if you want to.

What is your most immediate possession? What is point of contact with the universe? What is it through which every experience is either translated or expressed? *Your body.* Yet how often are you clearly aware of it? How often do you experience yourself as a physical organism in space?

Modern men live almost entirely in their minds. Their center of gravity is in their heads. A person who is more emotional and sensitive to human beings has a center of gravity that is lower down, in the heart or the solar plexus.

In Eastern countries they believe that the center of gravity should be in the lower belly. The Japanese use the word "Hara" to describe the balanced individual who is centered in this way. This exercise is designed to help you get a taste of what such a lower sense of gravity would be like as a more permanent condition.

Close your eyes. Pay attention to your own breathing. Don't attempt to change it in any way. Just be aware of your breath moving in and out. Sense the changes that occur as your breath goes through this recurring cycle. Feel the warmth spread through your body . . . Sense that as you breathe in you are absorbing oxygen which helps you create new energy . . . Sense as you breathe out that you are expelling poisons your system has discarded . . . Do this for a minute . . .

Now visualize a light rubber ball in a hollow tube . . . When you breathe in, the ball rises to the top of the tube. When you breathe out, it sinks. Watch the ball going up and down as you breathe in and out . . .

See the tube as inside your body. When you breathe in, the ball rises all the way up into your head. When you breathe out, it sinks.

Each time you breathe out, visualize the ball as sinking further. Each time you breathe in, see the ball as rising less high . . . Let the ball slowly sink as it moves back and forth . . . Take as long as you want until the ball settles into the pit of your stomach, midway between your belly button and your sex organs . . . Don't force it. Let it settle down at its own pace. Keep breathing quietly . . . As the ball settles, feel it as a warm presence. Let its warmth spread through your lower belly . . . Let your consciousness settle to that spot. Let your experience, your sensations, arise from that spot . . . Your lower belly is the center of the universe.

Try saying that to yourself silently. "The lower belly is the center of the universe." Experience what happens to you when you do this . . . Continue to breathe. Continue to experience from there. Try to listen to my voice from there. Try to sense your body from there. When you open your eyes, try to see the world from there.

This is the process of centering. In Zen Buddhism this process is basic to all further training. But do not think about it. Sense it.

Ask yourself, "As I experience the world from this low center of gravity in myself, am I afraid of being overwhelmed by the encounter experience?" You should get a very direct and immediate answer. Do you?

Frank: Yes, I do. There is nothing to be concerned about. Emotions are like leaves in the wind. They blow past me and settle on the ground.

John: I feel like a fool. Why didn't we do this before?

Richard: We didn't need to.

Marcia: I don't think I quite get it. Maybe I am thinking about it too much. Was I supposed to feel as if I were pregnant?

Richard: Did you?

Marcia: Yes, but then I began to feel anxious. So I guess it didn't work.

Richard: Where did you feel anxious?

Marcia: My heart started beating and my stomach contracted.

Richard: And you probably started imagining some situation.

Marcia: Yes.

Richard: So you weren't really centered in your lower belly. You were in your emotions and your head. If you are down there, you can't be afraid. There may be fear in you, but you don't have to be touched by it. Does anybody else want to say anything?

—I don't know how much of this I can take.

Marcia: I was wondering whether you would ever say anything. Who are you?

—My name is William Westerfield.

Marcia: How about Bill?

Bill: All right. I am really up-tight. I thought this was going to be a good experience for me but I just don't like it. You people are all right. I don't have anything against you, but I just can't turn myself inside out like most of you. I just want to get out of here. Frankly, I intended to take off before lunch.

Marcia: But you didn't.

Bill: Maybe I am too stingy to waste the money. I did ask Richard if I could get a partial refund.

Marcia: What did he say?

Bill: That I could leave if I wanted, but he wasn't going to reward me for running away. So here I am and hating every minute of it.

Ann: Is there anything you would like us to do for you?

Bill: Hit me over the head. Dope me up. I just don't want to be conscious. I would love to fall asleep and wake up Monday morning safe at home in my bed.

Richard: Do you have your own bedroom?

Bill: Of course.

Richard: Do you sleep there alone?

ton, are you sure? Would you three lie down next to Bill and hug him? Don't suffocate him, but hold him to you. And you, Bill, let the trembling come out.

Bill: How can I do that?

Richard: It is already inside you. Relax and let it show on the outside. You don't have to do a thing but allow it. Don't be afraid or ashamed. And Penny and John and Thurston, help him feel secure enough to do it. Let it come through in just one place, an arm, your neck. Then let is spread . . . Let it feel like a wave or a small convulsion . . . Let it take you. There is nothing that can happen . . . You are protected . . . That's it. Let it come. Let it grow. It shouldn't be held in . . . You want to express it, to be rid of it at last. Let it come through you and leave you . . . Make a sound if that will help. Moan, or cry out, or scream. Let your body loose.

Bill slowly begins to tremble in his arms and legs. His teeth chatter. Then his neck begins to twitch. Slowly his whole body becomes involved.

Richard: Keep breathing. Keep breathing. And make a noise.

Bill makes a banshee sound, wavering and haunted. He gasps for breath and begins to quiet down.

Richard: Help him to relax. Talk to him. Stroke him. Breathe on him.

Thurston: Breathe?

Richard: Warm him with your breath.

Bill: I am . . . all right. It isn't necessary.

Richard: Stay where you are. Accept some help. You don't have to prove how strong you are. It took guts just to let all that come out.

Penny: We are all here. Nothing can happen to you.

Bill: I know that. I am really all right. Just give me some room to breathe.

Richard: Give him room.

Bill: Was that a hysterical attack?

Richard: Does it matter?

Bill: I'm interested.

Richard: It began deep inside you as a hidden fear. Then it started to emerge as an emotion. Finally it came out into the open. Now you can be free of it.

Bill: The last time I felt anything like that was in the army.

Frank: What happened?

Bill: I was trapped in cross fire. I couldn't go forward and I couldn't retreat. The Communists knew I was there. They were patiently waiting for me to show myself. There was nothing to do but wait, knowing that they might attack at any time if they thought my company had withdrawn. I was there until nightfall. I couldn't stand it any longer in the dark. I made it back to our lines. When I got there a grenade went off where I had been. They must have sent a man crawling through the mud to blow me up. That was when I went to pieces. I trembled for a day and a half without stopping. When I woke up I was trembling. I must have trembled in my sleep. I was so cold. At the end I developed a fever and shivered with that for two days. Then I was all right. But I don't think that a sense of bitter cold and fear ever really left me.

Richard: How long ago was that?

Bill: Three years ago. Why?

Richard: Just curious. How do you feel now?

Bill: A little feverish. I was chilly last night. Could I just lie down in a blanket for a while?

Penny: Here. I brought mine to the meeting. Do you want an aspirin?

Bill: No. Nothing. That would just make me cold again . . .

John: What happens now?

Richard: Does anybody have anything they want to deal with?

Silence.

Richard: How about a change of pace then? Let's try some theater games.

Ann: What is that—like charades?

Richard: No, theater games are exercises originally developed to train actors in improvisation.

Frank: What is the point?

Richard: The best answer is to experience them for yourself. In general they help a person be more flexible and have greater control over his own behavior. Shall we try one? Everyone who wants to try, get up. When I say "go," I want you to start moving around the room in slow-motion, as slow as you can. When I say "regular," move at a normal pace without any break. When I say "slow," go back to the original pace. That is all. Any questions?

Marcia: Do you mean slow-motion with arms and legs?

Richard: With everything—breathing, eye movements, even heartbeat, if you could do it. Get ready. Slow-motion first. GO . . . REGULAR . . . SLOW . . . and stop . . . How was that?

Marcia: Slow-motion was like swimming underwater. I became very aware of every little action.

Richard: That is what is supposed to happen.

Frank: I had trouble. My legs were all right, but I couldn't slow my breathing and blinking and all that. It just made me anxious to try and then you suddenly said "regular" and I gave a big jerk. I couldn't make a smooth transition.

Richard: How do you most like to move?

Frank: I don't understand what you mean.

Richard: Is it easier and more enjoyable for you to move quickly or slowly?

Frank: I guess I like strong movement.

Richard: Slow-motion goes against this tendency. Each of us has a vocabulary of motions. In some areas we are well-developed. In others not. If we were dancers we would have to correct our weaknesses. As people we can let it slide. But if we cannot move strongly and weakly, it is like being able to feel love without knowing hate. It is one-sided and incomplete. Shall we try something else?

Marcia: Why not!

Richard: Since you are so eager, why don't you pick two other people to work with?

Marcia: John and Ann.

Richard: Good. Will the three of you stand about five feet apart and move slowly toward a central spot, which you all seek to occupy? Move in slow-motion and do not touch one another while trying to enter the central position.

Frank: But that is impossible. How can they do something that is impossible?

Richard: Just try it and see what happens. Are you ready? No talking until it is over. BEGIN.

They come slowly together. They move as if against a resistance, or as if they were weightless, engaging in graceful contortions designed to help them occupy the center without touching each other. The group watches with growing interest. John, Ann, and Marcia are completely absorbed. Ann sinks down and attempts to enter the center from below. Marcia tries to walk in. John uses a spiraling motion.

Richard: Get as near the center as you can and come to rest . . . Hold the position for a few seconds . . . That's all.

Thurston: That was beautiful to watch. How did it feel to be in it?

Ann: It was really interesting. At first I was very aware of what I was doing, but then I realized that unless what I was doing related to what John and Marcia were doing, it wouldn't work. It had to be one movement from three people. I wouldn't say we got there, but I felt what it might be like if we had.

Richard: What about doing an impossible task, Frank?

Frank: Well, it was impossible. I was right. Three bodies cannot occupy the same space. But I guess that wasn't the point, was it?

Richard: What do you think the point was?

Frank: I am not sure. You put them in a position where they had to act in a new way in order to find any kind of resolution.

Richard: If you ask a person to do something that is impossible within his own frame of reference, the only way he can approach it successfully is to change his frame of reference. In this case a person must redefine the three separate bodies as one organism of which he is a part. He must change his sense of identity.

Ann: I understand that.

John: That was a sort of Koan in motion.

Frank: What?

John: That's a Japanese riddle used by Zen masters to train their students. They always involve unanswerable questions like "How do you clap one hand?"

Richard: Both of these exercises have one common element that always exists in theater games—a point of concentration. Sometimes there is more than one point. In both exercises you had to concentrate on moving in a certain way. In the second you had, in addition, to remember not to touch.

Let's try something of a different nature in which the point of concentration is on something that doesn't exist. Ann, pick a partner.

Ann: I'd pick Bill but he is down for the count. How about you, Frank? You have a vivid lack of imagination.

Frank: Are you sure you want me?

Ann: Sure. I like to have obstacles to overcome.

Richard: The two of you are shortly going to discover something in the middle of the room. It can be anything. The only

limit is that it should be no bigger than the inside of a tennis
ball. Your task is to relate to it as realistically as possible. Let the
situation develop in any way that seems natural. Start whenever
you want, but no preplanning. You must both discover it together . . .

Ann looks intently at a spot on the rug. Frank watches her,
looks at the spot, shakes his head, looks at her again.

Frank: I didn't do it.

Ann: Who said you did?

Frank: You usually jump to conclusions. What are we going
to do about it?

Ann: We could cut it out.

Frank: That would be just great. How would the rug look
with part of it cut out? Anyway I think it would spread.

Ann: Couldn't we pour alcohol on it?

Frank: What good is that going to do? Let's scrape up as
much as we can.

Ann: Are you going to touch it?

Frank: Oh, come on. I need something to scrape with.

Ann: Here, use my nail file, only don't give it back to me.

Frank scrapes at the spot and collects the scrapings in his
hand, goes to a window and empties what he has picked up.

Frank: I think I better wash my hands. I'll be right back.
(He leaves.)

Ann: I wonder if I should tell him how my great-uncle got
leprosy. It was nice of him to volunteer to clean it up, but what's
the use? It is only going to spread, once it starts. I suppose the
rug could be burned but it must be in the walls. The whole
group must be infected, but I won't tell them. They would only
panic . . . Did you get them good and clean, Frank?

Frank: As clean as I can.

Ann: That was a brave thing to do.

Frank: Somebody had to do something. But should we tell

them? Would it do any good? If the Board of Health heard about it they would only quarantine the group. We might be here together for months. That would really be something.

Ann: Why don't we forget about the whole thing? Maybe it will die.

Frank: Do you believe that?

Ann: No.

Frank: How can we let people leave here? They will only infect others.

Ann: What can we do?

Frank: I don't know. I wish I had never seen it. I don't know what to do . . . That's it.

Richard: Very good. What was it that you saw?

Ann: A fungus growth.

Frank: It was a mushroom, really hideous colors, purple, orange, and bright pink vomit.

Ann: I saw darker shades. It kept changing shapes. It was alive and clinging. I was afraid if I touched it that it would penetrate into my skin and never let go.

Richard: Where did it come from?

Frank: I didn't want to find out. What did it all mean?

Thurston: I would say that you are afraid that what we are exposing to one another may end up poisoning us all and, far from becoming improved, that we may end up unfit for human society.

Ann: But I don't feel bad. I feel better now, as if I had been sick to my stomach and thrown up.

Richard: You cannot get frozen at any one stage. If the group weren't constantly shifting and growing, such a fantasy would never be generated. This very movement enables us to handle it.

Thurston: I have had enough.

Marcia: Me too.

Frank: I am up to here in group.

Richard: It is about 4:30. Why don't each of you spend a period of time completely by yourself? Don't speak to anyone for a half an hour or longer. But don't just sit and ruminate. Do things you don't usually do by yourself. Run, scream, talk to yourself, or meditate if that is unusual for you. But get away from everyone else. I will see you all at supper, providing you don't get lost in the woods . . .


*Saturday late afternoon*

(I was alone last night. I've been in the woods with John. Now I am alone in the woods by myself. Last night I wanted to be a bear. It would feel silly to get down on all fours. Someone might see me. I need to get further away. Maybe I could run . . .

(I have got to rest . . . This place looks far away from everything. "Hello!" No answer. "Come out. I want to kill you!" No answer. Oh well, some people are just not friendly . . .

(I feel very uneasy. It is spooky here. There are animals watching me. Keep away. I bite. I scratch. I could tear your throat out. Wow! Is that little old me talking? Mushy Marcia, the all-American sweetheart. I want to claw at the ground and dig a hole . . . and sniff the earth . . . that is a beautiful smell . . . I want to lick the earth . . . Eawwww . . . spit it out . . . chew on the particles I can't spit out . . . I want to roll in the earth . . . kick my legs out . . . bang with my arms . . .

(This must really look like something. "Is anyone watching?" No answer. There is never any answer . . . I feel like getting undressed. Now that would be stupid. If somebody comes along . . . I'll take off my shoes and socks . . . and my blouse . . . and skirt . . . that's enough . . . boy, am I jumpy. I hope nobody comes along and discovers what a sex maniac I am . . . I wish everyone would come along . . . I really do, and I could say, here I am. Here I really am. My cheeks are flushed.

(What was that? That was definitely something. "Is anyone there?" Maybe it's just a squirrel or a falling branch. Maybe it is John or Frank. I feel embarrassed. I want to cover myself up. "If there is anyone there, would you please have the decency to say so!" Nothing.

(It would be so simple to get dressed, or to get undressed completely. Then I would be completely safe or completely vulnerable. I wonder if I dare. I know what I would really like to do . . . find the stream, get undressed and go in. That's what I'll do. But first a good shout. Yahhhhhhhhhh!"

(The water should be somewhere over here . . . It should be . . . there it is, totally deserted. That's wonderful. All right, Marcia. Now do it or forget about it . . .

(I am going to do it . . . Now! Here I am . . . in the middle of the forest . . . completely naked. I feel so free, but scared, like a deer sniffing for a hunter . . . My heart sounds like a tom-tom.

(There is the water . . . It is probably could . . . It is cold! . . . but in I go . . . splashing, kicking, shouting . . . It is so cold!

(If I had only brought a towel . . . This is a magic spot. I hadn't really looked at it before. The moss on the rocks. A little cave under the fallen tree, and the sound of the water. That is such a beautiful sound . . .

(I almost feel so at home . . . If I only didn't have to worry about people . . . And I don't even want to be alone. I could make love to someone now. I don't have to, but it could happen. Or I could just sit, feeling cold, my feet dangling in the water, leaning over seeing my blurred reflection in the moving stream.

(There are fish. They move so quickly in the shadows. How do I look to you? Someone from outer space. I heard of a garden made all of moss. I would love to be there and lie down on it, turning overly slowly, sinking down into it . . .

(I am getting cold and shivery. Too bad John isn't here to warm me up. I guess I am just going to have to run . . . Naked or not, here I come . . . Wheeeeeeeeeeeee . . . I can't stop laughing . . . What would my poor dead mother think? . . . Maybe she is smiling . . . I am so happy . . . Where am I? Wouldn't that be something—to be lost in the woods, naked, I can't exactly call for help.

(If I only had a compass. But I don't know which way I want to go. Oh, what the hell. The stream can't be far. If I climb something I should be able to see it . . . that big rock that's flat on top . . .

(Hmm. It is warm up here. The rock must keep the heat. If I didn't feel self-conscious I could lie down here . . . Why not? . . . I don't think I can be seen. The stream is on my right . . .

(I haven't done anything like this in twenty years . . . I never really did anything like this. It's not the same when you are a little girl. Nobody minds if you are naked. There is nothing bad about it, nothing to get embarrassed about . . .

(It is just a waste of time to think about it. I am here. The rock is warm . . . not comfortable, but warm. If I could only completely relax. For the next minute I am going to relax. After that I can get tense again . . . I can see myself up here . . . as if I were standing twenty-five feet away in the trees. It is really a beautiful scene. I look like an advertisement for White Rock . . . I look like a vestal virgin waiting to be sacrificed. A hooded figure will come and plunge a golden sword in my heart. I will tremble slightly, and my blood will drain slowly down the rock.

(I wouldn't mind. I would be happy to be sacrificed right now, while I am happy and free, if it would help anyone. If it would make the crops fruitful, or keep away plagues or make the rain fall . . .

(Making love is being sacrificed, in a way. That is a strange thought. It makes me frightened but fills me with a sense of anticipation. For what? For whom? It has never really been like that; not noble or a ritual.

(How long am I going to stay here? Someone is going to come sooner or later. Do I want to see anyone? Not now. I don't want to be touched. I only want to go back and get dressed and then quietly slip into my room and sleep before dinner time . . .)

# Saturday night

Bill: How long is this session going to last?

Richard: Why?

Bill: I want to go to bed early.

Richard: It will go on as long as there is any purpose. We can break at eleven or go on till two.

Frank: Or stay up all night, right?

Richard: Yes.

Bill: I was afraid of that.

John: Where is Marcia? She wasn't at supper.

Frank: Did anybody look in her room?

John: I knocked, but there was no answer.

Richard: Maybe she is asleep. Why don't you check?

John: All right, I'll be back in a minute.

Ann: Maybe she doesn't like the food.

Penny: Or the company.

Frank: How did you like the mushrooms for supper?

Ann: I thought I would throw up, but I made myself eat them. They were pretty good.

Frank: How are you doing, Thurston? You have been pretty quiet.

Thurston: What's wrong with being quiet? Is that a sin?

Frank: I was just wondering how you were doing.

Thurston: All right, I guess. I'm a little jumpy. I can't imagine why, such pleasant surroundings, congenial company, affable host. I guess I'm difficult to please.

Bill: I wonder if John is coming back.

Frank: He should if she wasn't in her room.

Bill: What about if she was?

Richard: I think they are coming . . .

Marcia: I fell asleep.

Frank: Is that how you spent your time alone?

Marcia: No, I was in the woods.

Bill: Asleep?

Marcia: No, naked.

Bill: You're kidding.

Marcia: Yes, I'm kidding.

Bill: Are you?

Marcia: You'll never know.

John: She's not kidding.

Bill: How do you know?

John: It was only a question of time.

Marcia: Until what?

John: Until you were running through the forest laughing and screaming, completely naked.

Marcia: You saw me.

John: I didn't see anything. I was busy with my own thing.

Marcia: What was that?

John: I was playing Hitler. I killed off 100,000 people.

Richard: What were you doing, Bill?

Bill: I was under my covers in my bed. I thought I would go to sleep, but I couldn't. I kept hearing the sound of the shells, and then the deathly quiet in between. Where were you?

Richard: I was in the steam room relaxing.

Ann: That's the first I heard about a steam room.

Richard: It is more like a sauna bath.

Ann: Why didn't you mention it before?

Richard: I thought you knew. It tells about it in the instructions you have in your room.

Ann: Who reads instructions?

Richard: If you had, you would have discovered there is a sauna in the basement.

Frank: How big is it?

Richard: Big enough.

Frank: For the whole group?

Richard: Yes, if necessary.

Frank: Well, that is something worth thinking about.

Marcia: Since I have been exposed, so to speak, I may as well ask a question that has been on my mind. What about nude marathons?

Richard: Is that addressed to me?

Marcia: Yes.

Richard: Then why were you looking at John?

Marcia: I wanted to see if he would smile . . . He didn't . . . Anyway, what about them?

Richard: They exist. Do you have a professional interest or are you asking about having one with this group?

Marcia: I was just curious . . .

John: About having one in this group!

Marcia: Oh, shut up!

Richard: What reactions do you all have to the question?

Bill: Sounds interesting to me.

Penny: Count me out.

Richard: I'm not asking whether you would be willing to participate. What reaction do you have to the idea?

Penny: I think Bill just wants to see naked women. I don't

want any part of that. If he has those needs, let him meet them somewhere else.

Ann: I wouldn't particularly like it, I don't think. But I wouldn't refuse if that was what everyone wanted. But I don't know what the point would be?

Bill: Are you kidding?

Richard: What would the point be, Bill?

Bill: That's a funny question, coming from you. I have heard things about these encounter groups.

Richard: What have you heard?

Bill: Oh, about orgies and things.

Richard: Where have you heard that?

Bill: I don't know. Rumors. I have seen some pretty wild things in magazines.

Richard: Is that what you came for?

Bill: I'm not a hypocrite. I thought I might make a connection. It's a good way to meet a willing female, whatever happens in the group.

Richard: Did you sleep alone last night?

Bill: That's none of your damn business. Anyway, tonight is a new ball game.

Richard: I'm not being critical. I admire your honesty.

Marcia: Are we going to have a nude marathon?

Richard: You are awfully anxious.

Marcia: I just think that if we are going to do it, we should do it. Why analyze it to pieces?

Richard: What do you think would happen? Why do you want it?

Marcia: I don't know exactly. I just want to have the feeling I had when I was alone, with a group. I honestly don't know what to expect. Maybe we would all sit around and be embarrassed. It might stop everything dead.

Thurston: I don't mean to revert to my old character. But isn't this whole thing rather childish? It reminds me of when I was seven years old and the boys and girls went out in the woods to have a peeing contest.

Marcia: Who won?

Thurston: I'm sure I don't remember. That wasn't the point. We were little kids curious about the difference between boys and girls. That was a long time ago. I am not curious anymore . . . What is the purpose of a nude marathon anyway?

Richard: It is no different from any other exercise or experience we go through. People get undressed as an experiment, to see how it affects their behavior. It is hard to be dignified in the nude. It is a way of stripping away all roles. Everyone is equal . . . It is also a way of focusing on how people feel about their own bodies and those of other people. It depends a lot on who does it and for what purpose. If the people involved really want to have an orgy, they don't need a nude encounter to set it off. Orgies have been going on throughout recorded history. They aren't a modern invention. Sitting in a group naked can make you much more up-tight.

Marcia: It doesn't sound like so much fun anymore. Why does everything have to be clinical?

Richard: We have all been undressing ever since we got here, intellectually and emotionally. Taking off your clothes is a part of the process in a symbolic sense. There is nothing being hidden and consequently nothing any longer to be ashamed of in theory. In fact, being naked brings you face to face with feelings you might otherwise avoid.

Thurston: I always understood that society was created in part to help control sexual feelings. If people gave rein to their impulses, everyone would be promiscuous.

Richard: Is that how you feel?

Thurston: No. But I am an older man, happily married. I am

sure that I would behave quite properly with any of the women here if I were alone with them.

Richard: I am sure you would too. But are you attracted to any of them?

Thurston: Why, all of them. That is my point.

Richard: You mean if the conditions were right and no one would be hurt that you might have sexual relations with any woman here?

Thurston: Is that so strange?

Richard: No. How do you feel, Marcia?

Marcia: Why pick on me?

Richard: You brought the whole thing up, indirectly. How do you feel about the men here?

Marcia: Differently.

Richard: Can you imagine yourself going to bed with them?

Marcia: One at a time or all at once?

Richard: That is entirely up to you.

Marcia: What about you?

Richard: How do you mean?

Marcia: Should I consider you?

Richard: Do you want to?

Marcia: Do you want me to?

Richard: Do you want me to want you to?

Marcia: You are so damn frustrating. YES!

Richard: Why didn't you say so?

Marcia: Because I am a woman and I wanted you to say so. Anyway, yes, I can.

John: While we are being honest about it, I can picture some pretty wild scenes. I don't know that I want to describe any of them. I am getting scared by this whole thing. Do you really know what you are doing, Richard?

Richard: If *I* were doing it, I would be more concerned. If underneath I really wanted strongly to have an orgy, then I could subtly lead you toward that end, whether it would be healthy and good or not. That is something I have to worry about quite a lot. If you want to know whether I am scared . . . Yes, I am. The ground under me is shaky. But I know from past experience that as long as I am uneasy or scared, nothing bad is likely to happen. Everything is relative. If we were writing a novel, we wouldn't think twice about including an orgy, or committing a murder. If we were acting on a stage, it would still be acceptable. If we improvise with each other, it begins to get more threatening. If we talk about it as real people, more threatening still. If we do it, then it is most threatening of all. Yes, all these things have happened in reality, only not to us, or if they did, we cannot remember them. We need to find a realm of experience somewhere between creative fantasy and everyday reality in which to experiment.

Frank: I wonder what would happen if we turned out the lights for five minutes and began to walk around.

Bill: What could happen in five minutes?

John: Suppose we left the lights on and for five minutes everybody did exactly what they wanted to do?

Ann: I couldn't do that!

John: Why not?

Ann: I wouldn't dare. Suppose I went up to you and hit you hard. You would probably hit me back and hurt me. I don't want to be hurt. So I probably wouldn't hit you in the first place.

John: You could only be natural if I wasn't.

Ann: Yes.

Richard: There are a number of ways we could go right now. I want to suggest that we go all the way, but in fantasy.

Bill: I don't want . . .

Penny: Oh, shut your dirty mouth!

Richard: Everybody be quiet. Shut your eyes and relax. For the moment you don't have to decide anything. Forget what we have been talking about. Pay attention to your breathing and your heartbeat . . . Sink into your own sensations . . .

Now, when you are ready visualize the members of this group as you last saw them. Only this time they are all naked. For the next five minutes imagine what happens. I will let you know when the time is up . . .

The room is completely silent. Occasionally someone sighs. Everyone appears absorbed in what they are doing . . . Marcia laughs . . . Bill coughs . . .

Richard: The time is up. Open your eyes. Anyone want to say anything?

Marcia: Why did you interrupt me?

Richard: What were you doing?

Marcia: I was being chased by Frank, Bill, and John in the forest.

Bill: What happened before that?

Marcia: We played games. We imitated each other.

Bill: Are you putting me on?

Marcia: No. What happened to you?

Bill: Do I have to spell it out?

Richard: What did happen?

Bill: I made out with the women.

Richard: Which ones?

Bill: Oh, come on. What difference does it make?

Richard: It might to the women.

Bill: Penny and Ann.

Richard: How did they react?

Bill: They loved it, especially Penny.

Richard: How do you feel now?

Bill: I feel angry.

Richard: At whom?

Bill: At Marcia. She wouldn't have anything to do with me. I told her I would force her and she laughed at me.

Penny: Good for her. You really are a creep. If you came near me I would scream . . . Just don't try it. If I get scared I can be violent.

Richard: Anyone else?

John: We sat around talking as if nothing had happened and then suddenly Ann pointed her finger at you and said, "Richard has nothing on." We all looked around and discovered we were in the same condition. Then we decided that if we all held hands we would be safe. We held hands and looked at each other. Then Thurston got an erection and was very embarrassed and the girls made various complimentary remarks which only made it worse. Then a funny thing happened. Bill turned into an old spinster and started lecturing us, saying how naughty we were being. She (he) was going to send us to bed without supper when you broke in.

Ann: I had a strange experience. It was really unpleasant. We were all here undressed, looking around and waiting to see what would happen next. Nobody wanted to make the first move. Then you suddenly reached up near your neck and started to unzip your skin. You had a zipper that went straight down the front. You took off your skin like a sweater. Underneath were blood vessels, muscles, fat, and various organs. Other people started doing the same thing. Then you started taking yourself apart. I remember when you reached in and took out your heart. You had all the various parts in front of you neatly arranged, and everyone was copying you. In the end we all sat there, a circle of upright grinning skeletons and Marcia asked you, "Is this a nude marathon?"

Richard: What did I answer?

Ann: You said, "No, we still have bones on," and you started to take them apart. You hadn't completed dismantling yourself when you stopped the exercise.

Richard: Anyone else?

Silence . . .

Richard: Then I want to suggest that we drop the subject for the moment. If there is an interest in meeting without clothes, then I suggest that whenever we finish here those who want to, go to the sauna. But we don't have to decide anything about it now . . . There is one thing I am concerned about, three things actually . . . the three people who have not said anything so far. No one has made an issue of it and my theory has been that it can be just as hard to be quiet as to talk, so I left them alone. But the situation has gone far enough. I am sure you people have talked to one another and to others, but not when the group has been meeting as a whole. I suggest that the three of you sit in the center of the group and talk together about your feelings in this situation.

—I really don't want to.

—I will if you think it is necessary.

—I was wondering how long I could get away with it.

Richard: Sit in a small circle facing each other and we will sit around you.

—My name is Norma. Who are you?

—Alan. And you?

—Sheila. What are we supposed to do? I feel very conspicuous.

Norma: I am just plain frightened.

Alan: I usually talk a lot. I was in a group before and they really jumped on me for hogging the limelight, so I decided to keep my mouth shut as long as possible this time. My jaw is sore just from keeping it closed.

Sheila: I am all right when I am with one other person. I had a great talk with Frank. But I just freeze up in front of a group. I was in a play in the third grade. I came out on stage and forgot every single line. It was awful. They had to read them to me. I finally ran off the stage in tears.

Norma: I don't know what I am doing here. I don't understand what is going on. All these outbursts just frighten me. I think it is terrible.

Alan: What do you think is the purpose?

Norma: I told you. I don't know. I just hope I make it through tomorrow.

Alan: How do you feel about me?

Norma: You are all right, I suppose. But you have been in this sort of thing before, so I don't really understand you. How could anyone possibly want to come back?

Alan: You strike me as a very simple little girl who wants to meet a nice man, get married and raise a family.

Norma: What's wrong with that?

Alan: Nothing, I suppose. Isn't there anything else you want?

Norma: I grew up believing that was what women were meant to do. I don't want anything else.

Alan: Maybe you are right. You shouldn't be here. You don't really care about yourself.

Norma: Why don't you leave me alone?

Alan: One last question. Are you religious?

Norma: Yes, I am.

Alan: Is it a traditional once-a-week type religion or something more fundamental?

Norma: I don't know exactly what you mean. It is fundamental to me.

Alan: All right. Forget about it. None of my business anyway. No reason you should change.

Norma: I believe everyone should change. Men are very weak creatures. They must always strive to perfect themselves.

Alan: That's what we are here for.

Norma: This? I don't mean this. I mean living a life according to the Commandments. You seem to want to break most of them.

Sheila: I don't mean to offend you, Norma, but when you start talking religion I go a little wild. If ever there were a bunch of sick hypocrites, you find most of them in churches. The only good thing I can say about religion is that, thank God, it is dying!

Norma: I knew it. You are all atheists.

Alan: You don't know what anyone is. You certainly don't know what I am.

Norma: I think you are a devil's advocate. You are clever, but I don't think you are good.

Alan: How can you tell?

Norma: I can pray and ask for guidance.

Alan: Have you been praying?

Norma: That is mainly what I have been doing.

Alan: And what answer have you received?

Norma: Prayer isn't like sending a telegram. I just pray for help and protection.

Alan: It doesn't seem to be doing you much good right now.

Norma: God will protect me. He always has.

Sheila: If there were a God, don't you think that he would have something better to do than protect a sniveling female?

Norma: You don't understand. He loves those who worship him.

Sheila: I very much doubt it. He must have some standards.

Norma. I don't know why you are being so nasty to me. I haven't done anything to you.

Sheila: That's true. I am a little nuts on the subject of religion. I can't help attacking you when you come out with those ignorant brainwashed phrases. It just irritates the hell out of me.

Alan: You must have had a bad experience, Sheila.

Sheila: My father was a minister.

Norma: Oh, my God!

Sheila: Don't get the wrong idea. He is a wonderful man. I really love him. He was a bastard in some ways, but I really love him.

Norma: I wish you wouldn't curse your father, especially because of his calling.

Sheila: I am not cursing him. I curse those who tried to destroy him. He was a bastard in some ways. But then, who isn't? Just because you reverse your collar doesn't purify your soul.

Norma: What did your father do? Wasn't he a good man?

Sheila: He committed adultery.

Norma: Then he was evil. For a minister that is a terrible sin.

Sheila: Look, he was my father. He had needs. My mother was like you. She never let herself see what was happening. But I knew. It hurt me, I don't deny that, but I came to understand it. He never got involved with members of his congregation.

Norma: I understand your feelings about religion now. I can really sympathize. I might feel the same myself.

Sheila: You don't understand in the slightest. You would condemn him to hell with a smile on your face and a righteous glow in your heart. I understand you, but you don't understand me.

Alan: What was so good about your father?

Sheila: He really cared about people. He wasn't just a figurehead standing in front of the congregation on Sunday and visiting ladies' teas. He believed that the purpose of the ministry was to save souls. I am not talking about some phony conversion. I mean really getting down where people lived and working with them in their troubles and bringing God into their lives.

Norma: But you don't believe in God.

Sheila: He does. I did. I don't now. If there is a God, either we are his amusement or he just doesn't care. He is bored with his creation. Maybe he is busy on other projects.

Anyway, my father believes. He tried to make his whole life a testimony to that belief. If there is a need, he responds. He doesn't hold back anything for himself. But there is one sin of which he is guilty. He doesn't follow the rules. He sees people he shouldn't see. Gets involved in activities which the church board doesn't approve of. The young students don't come to church much anymore, so he goes to them. Sits with them in their meetings, participates in their sessions, attends their strike calls. The community doesn't approve of this social action. He is supposed to be in his church.

Have you ever read *The Brothers Karamazov?*

Norma: No.

Sheila: It contains a parable in which Christ comes back to earth during the Grand Inquisition. You know what happens to him?

Norma: No.

Sheila: He gets burned at the stake or crucified, I forget which. Nobody wants a true minister of God. They are too threatening and too revolutionary.

Norma: Where is your father now?

Sheila: In a small town in Illinois, in exile. They can't throw him out, but they are effectively stifling his influence.

Norma: I would like to meet him. He sounds like a good man, even if he does some terrible things.

Alan: Suppose I were to play Sheila's father? Would you be willing to talk to him right now?

Norma: That would just be play-acting.

Alan: I don't think so. I have met such a man. Let's try it. There is nothing else happening. Suppose you have asked to see me and we are talking in my study.

Norma: All right.

Alan as minister: I understand you are a friend of my daughter.

Norma: No. I met your daughter at an encounter group. She talked about you and I said I would like to meet you. I happened to be passing this way so I called for an appointment, and here I am.

Minister: Yes. I see. How was Sheila?

Norma: All right, I suppose. I really don't know.

Minister: I worry about her.

Norma: She seems to love you. She is terribly bitter about what has been done to you.

Minister: And you think she is wrong?

Norma: I think you are probably a good man with a terrible flaw.

Minister: It sounds as if Sheila has been talking.

Norma: I assume everything we say is confidential?

Minister: With the turn this conversation is taking, I certainly hope so. What is it you really want to talk to me about?

Norma: This may sound very presumptuous on my part, but I am concerned for your soul.

Minister: I see.

Norma: We do not share the same religion, but for any religion it is far worse for a minister or priest to commit a sin than for an ordinary person.

Minister: So they say. We must be above reproach.

Norma: But you don't really seem to believe it. I am sure, having met you, that you try to do good according to your own lights, but do you follow God's light? Do you obey his Commandments?

Minister: And you know what God wants?

Norma: It is all written down in the Holy Scripture.

Minister: The Scripture fulfills the essential of any venerated source. It allows for varied interpretation.

Norma: That is the word of the devil.

Minister: Do you think so? Am I in his service?

Norma: I pray that it is not so.

Minister: But you are not sure?

Norma: No, I am not. Knowing what I do about you, I cannot even feel safe as a woman.

Minister: You feel I might make some indecent proposition to you?

Norma: I don't know.

Minister: Rest at ease. I never get involved with a member of my congregation.

Norma: I am not in your congregation.

Minister: Are you sure that it is not I, but you, who desire such a thing? You would be surprised how many women dream of an affair with a minister. It combines earthly fulfillment with heavenly sanction.

Norma: No. No. That is an evil thought.

Minister: I did not say it was good, but you cannot dissolve evil by denying it. You end up by denying life. That—it is my first impression—is what you are doing.

Norma: I am sorry I came. I meant to be helpful.

Minister: And I end up trying to influence you against your better judgment. I must apologize. It is a minister's weakness to try and convert the faithless.

Norma: It is you who have lost faith.

Minister: You have no faith in human goodness, in the potential of humankind for growth. You must surround every natural function with fences, barbed wire, and machine gun implacements, lest anyone discover that what you call evil is natural, and that the book of rules which you defy is limited to a time, a place, and a culture. Nothing is absolute, my child. Even death is a matter of degree.

Norma: I am not as educated as you. I cannot argue. I can only pray for your soul.

Minister: And I for yours, my child. But I do not leave out your mind, emotions, your sensations, your sense of your own existence. I pray for all of you. I pray that you may discover that the world can exist without Commandments and that the only rivers are those which flow.

Norma: We cannot understand one another.

Minister: I understand you. You would understand me if you dared.

Norma: I suppose it is natural that my faith be tested. But I will not be found wanting. Thank you for seeing me. I am sorry that there was so little purpose to it.

Minister: Give my love to Sheila if you see her before I do. She must shock you even more than I. May you realize your heart's desire.

Norma: Good-bye. I am sorry if I sounded too harsh. Good-bye . . .

Sheila: That was very moving, Alan. You were really him. He is a wonderful fool. There are so few like him.

Alan: Why did you come to this group?

Sheila: My father had been getting some mail from a rightist religious group condemning encounter groups and sex education in the same breath. He said to me, "It must be good if they are trying so hard to destroy it. Why don't you go sometime if you have the chance?" So here I am, my father's emissary. I meant what I said, Alan. You were really good. I want to give you a big hug.

Alan: It will only shock Norma, but go ahead. I could use a reward.

She kisses him for almost half a minute. The room is completely silent.

Alan: You are some kisser.

Sheila: That is what I felt.

Alan: I should warn you that I am not your father. If you have been looking for a younger version of him, it ain't me. First of all, I am Jewish. Second, I have had some acting training. And third, I don't go for minister's daughters. They are too intent on being bad. They won't let it happen naturally.

Sheila: I thought you were.

Alan: Were what?

Sheila: Jewish. Don't worry. I am not after you. I think it is Norma you ought to be worried about.

Alan: You have got to be kidding.

Sheila: Do you have any idea what would happen if her defenses began to give?

Alan: I see what you mean. I could be both a father and a minister as well as someone of a different faith. She could really go to hell on the express route by falling for me. I'll be careful.

Norma: You two may find such talk sophisticated and amusing, but I think it is just bad taste.

Sheila: Suppose we have a truce. You leave my God alone and I will leave yours alone.

Norma: There is one question I wanted to ask you, Alan. What do you believe in?

Alan: Human sacrifice! I am a barbarian.

Norma: Be serious.

Alan: Actually I practice tantric yoga, the part about realizing God through sexual intercourse.

Norma: Is that true? Then you are perverted.

Alan: You don't even know what I am talking about.

Norma: Is that some Eastern form of excess?

Alan: No. It involves extraordinary control. But I don't mean to be so difficult. It is just that you are so tempting to bait.

What do I believe in . . . Growth, I suppose. What does any seed believe in? . . . the chance to become a plant, a flower, a tree. Does that sound very pagan to you?

Norma: I am getting a headache. The air is very close in here.

Alan: Nobody is trying to take your belief away from you, Norma. But anything anyone believes is bound to be tested if it comes out in the open. If it is as solid as you think it is, you have nothing to worry about.

Norma: I feel a little sick.

Alan: Would you let me hold you until you feel better?

Norma: Just don't touch me.

Alan: How about if Sheila and I both hold you? Nothing can happen. You are in front of a whole group of people.

Norma: This group wouldn't care what might happen. They might just cheer you on.

Alan: What do you think I have in mind?

Norma: I don't know and I don't want to know . . . some kind of wild orgy with two women. I am sure you have had such experience.

Alan: Let's not go into that right now. All I want to do is hold you until you feel better, like a mother might hold a child. Is that so terrible?

Norma: I suppose not. I always was suspicious. All right. If that is what is supposed to happen.

Alan and Sheila hold Norma, Sheila in the front and Alan in back. Norma is very stiff at first. Then she sighs and begins to relax. They begin to sway gently back and forth. Someone in the group begins to hum a lullaby. Others take it up. The sound gets louder . . . Richard joins the group in the center. One by one other persons move closer until everyone is huddled together with Norma in the middle, rocking gently back and forth.

Norma: I feel like a baby in her crib. I guess you are good people. I feel so scared.

Richard: Don't stop rocking. Why did you come to this group, Norma?

Norma: My mother wanted me to.

Richard: Your mother! You and Sheila really make a pair, her father and your mother.

Norma: They would get along just fine.

Richard: Your mother doesn't share your religious beliefs?

Norma: No. She and my father are divorced.

Richard: Does he?

Norma: No. He is even worse.

Richard: Who does?

Norma: Who does what?

Richard: Who shares them?

Norma: Everyone, my relatives, friends.

Richard: Everyone except your parents. Doesn't that bother you?

Norma: I don't care about my father. But I can't really understand Mom.

Richard: Most girls care about their fathers.

Norma: You don't understand. He is in a state hospital. Somehow I don't feel that he really exists anymore.

Richard: What about your mother?

Norma: I don't know. She seems happy. This is her sort of thing. She would enjoy it. I am just not like her, I guess.

Richard: Who are you like?

Norma: My grandmother, my aunt, lots of people.

Richard: What do you think is going to happen to your parents when they die?

Norma: That scares me sometimes. Don't they realize that after-death is forever? They just may not make it into heaven. But they won't listen to me. I am only their daughter. What parents ever listen to their children?

Richard: What does your mother say?

Norma: She says that she really appreciates my concern for her but that she doesn't look at things as I do.

Richard: Could you be your mother?

Norma: I thought you would ask that.

Richard: I want to ask you some questions about your daughter Norma. What is your name?

Norma as Mother: Silvia.

Richard: I have met your daughter, Silvia. She expressed some concern about your future life.

Silvia: Yes, she is kind of a religious nut.

Richard: You are not concerned?

Silvia: I grew up in the church and I grew out of it. I think there are good things about the church, but it can be very crippling too. It can take over your whole life. And some of their ideas about sex are terrible in this day and age. Their idea of a deadly sin is to have sex before marriage.

Richard: You don't agree with that?

Silvia: You have to be realistic.

Richard: Are you concerned about Norma?

Silvia: Not really. She has her life all planned out, just as the church recommends. There is nothing really wrong with it. I followed the same pattern myself. It just isn't enough. But if she is happy with it, I wouldn't take it away from her. Maybe she has to cling to something like that, to make up for the loss of her father. That's why I don't attack her faith. She needs something to depend on.

Richard: Why did you urge her to go to an encounter group?

Silvia: I hoped that her eyes might be opened to more of life. She is really very rigid for a girl of twenty, but I don't have too much hope. Anyway, I can't live her life. I have quite enough with my own . . .

Richard: Be yourself now. Are you in love at the present time?

Norma: No.

Richard: Are you attracted to any of the men in the group?

Norma: I suppose I feel the most for Alan, but that is because I have been involved with him. Why do you ask?

Richard: Could you imagine yourself making love to him?

Norma: I have never made love to anyone really. I never would unless we were married.

Richard: But you can imagine what it would be like?

Norma: No. I couldn't. I wouldn't want to. Don't you know that loving someone should be sacred? You make it seem so dirty.

Richard: I don't think so. Why do you have to equate imagining something with doing it? Is it so threatening to you? Are you that scared that if you relaxed a little, you would immediately fall into the abyss?

Norma: I think you are doing something evil. I can't help it. What is it you want me to do?

Richard: All that I asked is whether, in your imagination, you could dream of making love with Alan. I don't mean sleeping with, just engaged in a loving exchange.

Norma: I just can't.

Richard: Can't what?

Norma: Can't let myself do it.

Richard: If you felt it were all right, then perhaps you could?

Norma: But I know it isn't. I know that in my heart. Nothing you say can change my mind. If you continue then I will know for sure.

Richard: Know what?

Norma: That you are of the devil.

Richard: With you everything is a great theological drama. All right, let's play it your way. Suppose I am the devil. Then we will need an angel to protect you. Whom would you like?

Norma: Alan, I think.

Richard: Are you sure you can trust him?

Norma: I think he would play the part seriously. He wouldn't let his personal feelings interfere, whatever they are.

Alan: That's true. I wouldn't.

Richard: Where would you like this meeting to take place?

Norma: Just some place else; not here. It could be out in the forest. I am walking by myself and you two overtake me and we begin to talk. How would that be?

Alan: Fine, let's go.

Richard: You mean outside?

Alan: Why not? Everybody out. This should be interesting. Somebody grab a few flashlights. You can shine them on us.

The group streams out a side door, struggling with sweaters and light coats. They walk a short distance in the forest and Norma stops.

Norma: Right here. This is fine . . . It is so quiet . . . the air smells pure. I am thankful to get out of that room.

Richard as devil: What are you doing alone in the dark, my child?

Norma: Walking.

Devil: Don't you think that might be dangerous?

Alan as angel: She is not alone.

Devil: I see. Yes, well, that is different. What is your name, if I may ask?

Angel: What is yours?

Devil: In my feminine form I am called Lucy.

Angel: In mine, I am called Gabby.

Devil: Who is your friend?

Angel: Her real name is Norma. I call her Angela.

Devil: A revolting conceit. Tell me, young woman, do you think you are entirely safe with this fellow?

Norma: Entirely. He is an angel.

Devil: You mean he has been castrated?

Norma: I certainly wouldn't know about that.

Devil: Poor fellows. Their master believes in removing temptation.

Norma: And would I be safe with you?

Devil: I certainly hope not. What I mean to say is, doesn't a beautiful young creature like you, made as they say in a reflection of God himself, have something better to do than be guarded by this celestial eunuch?

Angel: If these insults are designed to make me angry and put me off my guard, you are wasting your time. This young girl will not be tempted. Even if she wavered, there are many others to watch over her.

Devil: What is the name of your prison, my dear? Do they give you your own number or do you share one with other room-mates?

Norma: I gladly follow the Commandments. I am not in prison.

Devil: There is nothing that tempts you then, nothing you desire which morality forbids?

Norma: I want to do good.

Devil: As we all do.

Norma: I have some doubts about you.

Devil: I have doubts about you also. Your convictions seem to be based on a combination of total lack of experience and a fanatic assumption that your truth holds for every living creature. You are an affront to the God who made you.

Norma: I have hurt no one. Why don't you leave me alone? I am content.

Devil: There is nothing in you hungry for understanding and experience? Why were you born?

Norma: To serve God.

Devil: Your God is dead.

Norma: That is absolutely ridiculous.

Devil: Ask your friend. See what he says.

Norma: Well?

Angel: You put me in an embarrassing situation.

Norma: Why? He is alive, isn't he?

Angel: I am not sure.

Norma: Do you have even the slightest doubt?

Angel: It's been so long since I've seen him. There have been rumors.

Norma: What sort of rumors?

Angel: An old chronic condition. He has stopped making public appearances. Some say he just is fed up with the whole thing.

Norma: I don't believe you. You are simply testing me.

Angel: That is not for me to do. I am here to protect you.

Norma: And this is how you do it, by undermining my faith?

Angel: I am an angel. I cannot lie, even to the devil.

Devil: Perhaps, my daughter, we should begin again. You have based your life on the existence of an all-knowing father, who has told you what to do, in a book every word of which you take to be holy.

Norma: Yes.

Devil: And now?

Norma: He exists. He must! You are both playing with me. You are torturing me.

Devil: Perhaps a new God is being born.

Norma: But if he is gone, whom do you serve?

Angel: You have hit upon a delicate point. In olden times when the master died, his servants and his wife died with them. But we seem to be very much alive. Perhaps he is also, just on an extended vacation.

Devil: Maybe he is having his face lifted.

Norma: I have been deserted. How can I trust either of you?

Devil: The point, my sweet young virgin, is that you cannot trust yourself. If you could, you would dispense with this elaborate claptrap with which you surround yourself.

Norma: Whom should I trust, you?

Devil: Do you have a better suggestion? I hope your faith in that unsexed companion of yours with the drooping wings has at least been shaken. He should be retired to a hairdressing establishment.

Angel: You take advantage of my disposition.

Devil: No. I am enjoying the suspension of celestial law that seems to have occurred in conjunction with God's temporary absence from the throne.

Norma: Then, I can do anything?

Angel: Be careful, my child. You are listening to the devil.

Norma: I have been listening to him all my life. But I never believed him, regardless of whom he spoke through.

Angel: The Commandments are eternal. Do not doubt them.

Devil: Do you really believe that?

Angel: Not exactly, but that is what I am supposed to say.

Norma: Just what is it you do believe?

Angel: Well, to be quite frank, I may look young, but I have been around for quite some time. My mind is not so sharp as it was. Sometimes I forget important scriptures. But I believe as you do, my child, that there is good and evil in the world. And that we must fight for the good. I have pledged myself. Only . . .

Norma: Only what?

Angel: When you have lived as long as I, you begin to lose the sense of just what is good.

Norma: Then how can you be an angel?

Angel: I do my duty as I have done it in the past. I sometimes have my doubts, like a policeman arresting the wrong man, but there must be angels even if they falter. No one is perfect.

Norma: I wonder why my mother left the church.

Devil: Your mother is a lovely woman, my child. Somewhat obstinate, but then it runs in the family.

Norma: Why don't you both go away and leave me alone?

Devil: Of course, my daughter, but is it safe alone in the dark?

Norma: It may not be safe, but that is what I want. Go away. Good-bye.

Angel: If you need me, pray, but make it loud. My hearing is not what it used to be.

Devil: May we meet again under more favorable conditions. Good-bye . . .

Norma: Is it over?

Richard: That is for you to say. I was asking you whether you could imagine yourself making love to Alan.

Norma: Yes, I could.

Richard: Would it be something good or would you be tortured by guilt?

Norma: I just don't know, but at least I can imagine it. Is that enough?

Alan: I don't want you to feel that this is supposed to lead to something. I understand what Richard is trying to do. I don't mind being used to help you open up, but I am not looking for anything to happen.

Norma: Don't be so worried. I am the one who is supposed to be worried.

Richard: And the rest of you out in the dark. Where are you? What are you thinking?

Marcia: I have cold chills running up and down my spine. It was so weird sitting here under the stars, listening to such a conversation. I haven't really thought about God in the last ten years. It never much mattered to me whether he existed or not. Right now I think he does.

Frank: Why is that?

Richard: Let's not get in a discussion. If you have a reaction give it directly.

Frank: I only asked because this whole thing had the opposite effect on me. I was quite religious when I was a teen-ager. Then I drifted away. This just gave me a great big push even farther. Freud was right. Religion is a neurosis. People who need it are looking for a big daddy. I pity Norma.

John: I pity you. Who are you kidding? You are still fighting the old man, just like Thurston. I kept wondering as I listened,

"Why do I like to run?" and I suddenly thought of that poem "The Hounds of Heaven." I am running from something bigger than I am, which I want to catch me. I have to run and I have to be caught. It sounds like a celestial love affair . . .

Thurston: Yes, I am fighting the old man, but my religious beliefs don't necessarily reflect that. Actually I am a pacifist. I don't believe in hate and killing. It never does any good. Norma is a young innocent child, rigid perhaps, with the light of a fanatic. Too bad in one so young. Still, there is nothing wrong with her beliefs. Quite like my own, if I had any. What I mean is that I just don't have very strong convictions anymore. Maybe I don't have the energy or the time, too many responsibilities . . .

Ann: When I was young my parents never made much of religion. I wanted to go to temple because my friends did, but I got bored. Later on when I came to this country I began to feel some lack. I became interested in mysticism. I joined a group that meditated. Sometimes we had seances. I still go sometimes. But I have lost interest. I am looking for something. Maybe it is a person, or an idea, or a belief. But there are so many of them. I just can't seem to find anything that lasts.

Richard: Have you had any drug experiences?

Ann: Are there any informers present?

Richard: If we want to blackmail each other, we already have plenty of material.

Ann: That's true. Yes, I've tried a few things—acid, pot.

Richard: And?

Ann: It was something. I suppose it was remarkable, but I didn't feel right about it. It was just an experience. I didn't feel I had earned it or that it related to anything else. I suppose I learned some things about myself. I could see how drugs could be useful, but people just take them for kicks . . .

Penny: I don't think I believe in anything. I'm not sure I want to. What is there to believe in? Science? Art? Love? Everything people put their faith in has an aspect which is horrible. Belief is a disease. I just wish I could learn to accept what is. That would be belief enough for me . . .

Richard: It is about half hour until midnight. A while ago I mentioned the baths. The time has come for you to decide whether you want to go. I don't want to make a big production about it. I certainly don't want anyone to go because they feel it is expected of them by the group. Go, if you go, because you want to, because you need to, or because you don't want to and think it would be good for you to force yourself. But take the responsibility on yourself. Don't put it on me, if you regret your action in the future . . . See you there at midnight, if you want to come.

# Midnight

Marcia: I wonder if everyone is going to come?

John: Do you plan to wear the giant bath towel around you indefinitely?

Marcia: How about that medium-sized towel you have around your middle?

John: Are you embarrassed?

Marcia: It doesn't feel quite natural. This isn't what I had imagined. I wonder where Richard is? We must be early.

John: Maybe he wants us to sweat it out on our own . . . Hi, Thurston!

Thurston: Do you two intend to sit there in your towels all night?

Marcia: I can see that you don't.

Thurston: If you are going into a sauna, you don't do it with clothes on.

Marcia: O.K. I will follow your example. Just don't start looking at me or I will feel like a fool . . . Hello, Frank. You are just in time.

Frank: For what?

Marcia: For the unveiling. Why don't we all count three?

Thurston: It is not warm enough in here.

Marcia: It feels pretty hot to me.

Thurston: No. The room is just slightly warm. It should be really hot, 190 degrees or so. I'll go check the thermostat.

Frank: Old Thurston really takes to this . . . You were going to count to three . . . Hello, Penny. You are in time for the general unveiling.

Thurston: In about fifteen minutes it will be warmed up.

Penny: Feels pretty hot right now.

John: If we wait for everybody to get here we will never take these towels off. Everyone for himself.

Penny: I'm glad that Bill isn't here. He would make me feel uncomfortable . . .

Frank: Hi, Bill. We were just talking about you.

Bill: Saying what?

Penny: I was saying I was glad you weren't here because you would make me uncomfortable.

Bill: That's tough. Why?

Penny: I don't want to be looked at as if I were a pin-up.

Bill: You just don't like being a woman.

Penny: That's not it. You just give me the feeling that you wouldn't care if my whole personality disappeared. In fact, you would prefer it, as long as my body were still functioning.

Marcia: Hello, Sheila. Is Norma coming?

Sheila: I doubt it. She would like to, but it is against her principles. She has some idea that this is going to be an orgy. And anyway, only her husband is supposed to see her naked.

Bill: Some orgy.

Marcia: How about if she wore a bathing suit?

Thurston: You don't go into a sauna bath in a bathing suit. It would clog your pores. You have to sweat.

Marcia: There are other things to consider than physical culture. Where is Ann?

Bill: I saw her talking with Richard. I guess she will be along. Hello, Norma. We didn't think you were coming.

Norma: I didn't think so either, but I won't stay unless I can wear my bathing suit.

Penny: Thurston may not approve, but wear whatever you want.

Thurston: You people just don't understand. The whole purpose of a sauna bath is to open the pores, purify the system, and help you to relax. If you wear clothes you can't get rid of the poisons.

Marcia: We get the message.

Thurston: Actually, after we are here for a while, we should take a plunge in cold water, or take a cold shower, then back in here for ten minutes and another shower. A wonderful experience!

John: You are quite a character, Thurston. It doesn't seem to bother you a bit that you are sitting around naked with a group of people engaged in encounter. Wouldn't your wife be concerned about that?

Thurston: But I go to the club twice a week to keep in condition.

John: Men and women?

Thurston: No. But what's the difference? A sauna is a sauna.

Richard: Spoken like a true Roman. Good morning, everyone. Ann will be right here. Is anyone missing?

Bill: Not yet.

Richard: Well then, we can begin.

Marcia: Begin what?

Thurston: Begin having the sauna, of course. But it isn't hot enough just yet. It will take another ten minutes to get up to the proper temperature. Of course I prefer hot rocks in the Swedish style myself.

Bill: Are you kidding?

Thurston: You don't even know what I am talking about.

Bill: Next you'll be telling me you peddle dope.

Thurston: The hot rocks are used to heat the sauna. That's all.

Ann: Hello, everybody. What a pretty bathing suit, Norma. When are you going to take it off?

Norma: I am not going to take it off and if everyone is going to make a big issue of it, I am leaving.

Richard: What do you think would happen to you if you did undress that won't happen anyway?

Norma: I don't want to talk about it. I don't want to stimulate anything.

Richard: Maybe you are wrong.

Norma: I wish I were.

Richard: Since you don't want to talk about it, let me ask whether there is anyone who thinks he or she could put himself in Norma's place and express how she feels.

Ann: I think I could.

Richard: Try.

Norma: I wish she wouldn't.

Richard: You are not responsible for what someone else thinks you think.

Norma: I was afraid something like this would happen.

Richard: Start!

Ann as Norma: Let's see. If I get undressed I will be defenseless. I don't think anyone will attack me but the whole group is going to get physically involved. Maybe it is all right for some of them, but for me it is a sin. This way I can be comfortable. I don't want to have to leave. But I must preserve some fine line of decency. I cannot tempt anyone. It wouldn't be fair. It wouldn't be right.

Richard: Is that how you feel?

Norma: Pretty close. You just won't be satisfied until you have me down on the floor with someone on top of me.

Richard: That is your idea, not mine.

Norma: But you think it, just the same.

Richard: Is that what you think, John?

John: I'm beginning to wish I could get the hell out of here. I don't like the atmosphere.

Richard: Anyone else?

Ann: As I was telling you in the hall, I am feeling quite anxious about the situation. (*pause*) You know, there is someone missing —Restas. I think of him because I had a horrible experience in a Nazi concentration camp. It will do me good to talk about it. (*pause*) I wonder what has become of Restas?

Bill: Maybe he went home. Were you really? Go on.

Ann: Did he go home?

Richard: Not that I know of. Only Thomas left and nobody seems to miss him. Does it matter?

Ann: I guess not. This incident. It was nothing much really. I was in a concentration camp and the guards used to amuse themselves. They would break in on the women taking showers and . . .

Richard: Would it help if we held hands? Sit in the center, Ann, on the stool.

Ann: And they raped us, that's all. It was nothing so special. Much worse things happened.

Norma: I think it is horrible.

Ann: The Americans did it too.

John: What was it like?

Ann: One just waited for it to be over. We knew they wanted us to fight back. So we didn't.

John: Did they hurt you?

Ann: Yes.

John: Sometimes I have fantasies of raping a woman but I never think of the woman's point of view.

Ann: It is not nice to be used as a piece of plumbing.

Thurston: You can't be as casual about it as you sound.

Ann: And then of course there were the hot showers which were used to open the pores so that the poison gas could work more quickly.

Richard: Focus on your feelings and sensations, Ann, not on your memories. What do you feel right now, in this place?

Ann: I feel like laughing.

Richard: Laugh then.

She giggles slightly hysterically.

Richard: What are you laughing about?

Ann: I think it is funny. All of you people sitting around naked in a hothouse listening to me tell about how I was raped. Don't you think it is funny? . . . Is that Restas now? Come in, Restas. Oh, Alan's with you. I was just telling about what the Nazi guards did to me in the shower.

Restas: Were you in a concentration camp? You do not have an accent.

Ann: That's a good question. Maybe this is all a fantasy. Maybe I dreamed about the guard throwing me on the floor and attacking me.

Restas: I am sorry to be late. I didn't know if I wanted to come.

Bill: Shut up and sit down. Go on.

Ann: Where is there to go?

Bill: What did it feel like?

Ann: I told you. I might have made it up.

Bill: I don't believe it. What was it like? Did you enjoy it? Come on. Be honest. How old were you?

Ann: I was fifteen. I had no choice. Those who refused were beaten up. I think they hoped I would refuse. Those men liked to hear people scream. It was the only way they could be sure they were doing their job.

Bill: You are holding out on me. What was it really like? I want to know.

Ann: I am sorry, little boy. You are not going to find out looking at girls in magazines and masturbating.

Bill: I can understand why they picked on you. You really are asking for it.

John: Leave her alone.

Bill: Are you her protector?

John: Just leave her alone. She has been through enough.

Ann: Please. Please. It is not necessary. This little boy doesn't bother me. If he and I were alone together here, he wouldn't know what to do.

Bill: That is about all I am going to take from you, you dirty whore.

Ann: That is right. It was my fault. I enjoyed it. They gave me special favors, cigarettes, candy, stockings. They even brought up my baby outside the camp.

John: You had a child?

Ann: If I am not making the whole thing up.

John: Where is he?

Ann: I am glad I don't know. Who cares? Probably dead. I don't feel so well.

Richard: What's wrong?

Ann: I want to throw up.

Richard: Go outside to the bathroom. If it doesn't happen by itself, stick your finger down your throat until it does. Come back when you feel better.

She leaves.

John: Some orgy, eh, Norma?

Norma: I feel terrible for her. She is so bitter. Men are such brutal creatures.

John: God damn it, how would you know? You keep yourself so wrapped up that you wouldn't know a man from a giraffe.

Norma: Isn't it true? Don't all men lust after women?

John: Don't you ever wonder about a religion that has to make so many things sinful? Just because I might be attracted to you doesn't mean that I have to do anything about it. It seems to me that women are much more interested in sex than men. It is their whole life. And while I think of it, if you think sitting there in a bathing suit makes you less tempting and less an object of attention, think again. You are the most conspicuous female in the group right now. Clothes may hide, but they also reveal, or half reveal. If you cared about the temptation to which you are subjecting us weak men, you would get rid of that suit. But you are a woman, a hung-up woman, but still a woman, you want to be noticed. You want to tantalize. That is O.K., but you ought to have the honesty to admit it.

Alan: I am concerned about Ann.

Richard: She will be back.

Alan: I know, but that must be a terrible thing to be reliving.

Richard: It is terrible to us living in a free country in peacetime. But for her it was more or less normal. One hundred years from now, living as we do might seem abominable.

Penny: You sound like a storm trooper. Don't you think it was wrong?

Richard: Every one of us continually gets hung up in the roles we play or those that are imposed upon us. It doesn't matter what they are. After a while we believe in them. A minister believes he is godly. A judge believes he is wise. A teacher believes he can teach. What they forget is that, given the conditions, any man can be a murderer, a rapist, a liar, a saint, a creative artist, a devoted husband. We avoid the roles that are too dangerous and enact those which are approved. But you are capable of evil. I am. I do not trust the man who denies it. I do not trust the man who is out of contact with those sides of himself. It is terrifying but it is true. We hide this truth under layers of deceit, boredom, and decay, but stripped away by war, famine, emergency, the truth emerges. We are all murderers. You had better believe it. Some of us do it in anger and jealousy. Others through indifference and denial of pain. But we kill each other and destroy ourselves quietly and systematically.

Ordinarily no one suspects. Under the conditions in which you are now, it is easier to see it. The lengths that people go to defend themselves against the truth that everyone else recognizes, is extraordinary. I feel for Ann. I feel for the indifference, the toughness with which her scar has healed. I long for her to face that which she has encapsulated, so that she is rid of it at last—the hate, the contempt, and the desire. But I would be lying if I denied that I can understand the guards. What man has not dreamed of violating women, enjoying both the sex and pain? It doesn't mean that I would do it directly, though maybe I would if there were no penalties involved, if society approved. Who can know unless faced with the situation? Most men will kill in war and feel completely justified. There is only one solution: to accept everything. I do not mean in an objective sense, but as an artist, as a god who has set this world in motion and who recognizes a pattern in the chaos.

Marcia: So that is what you believe.

Richard: A human being is a center of strong forces, much stronger than we dream. If they are let loose, he may be destroyed by them or driven mad. But if he is prepared—and that is what education should be—then he can face these forces and use them. This is maturity and this is strength. If I can allow myself to look at the women in this group and feel a sexual flash, I am in contact with a power. It can take me or I can control it. If I can hold this energy and let it grow, let it permeate my whole being, it will feed me. If I grow afraid, if I fear I might lose control, go wild, be rejected, look ridiculous, then I am in trouble. If I become involved with a particular woman, then the force has me. I am its victim. Similarly with the men. If I look around and react to the masculine bodies, feel an interest and admiration and an attraction; if I can do this without becoming concerned about my own masculinity or latent homosexuality; if I can accept it because it is there, then I can tap another aspect of sexual energy. I can bathe in this energy rather than be frightened of it. It can feed me rather than abuse me.

Marcia: I begin to understand you a little bit. You haven't had very much reality up to now.

Richard: You have to realize my responsibility. Whatever I do becomes a standard, whether I want it to or not. If I come over to you or you to me and we embraced, it would set a precedent. It would imply that I approve. Everything I do when I am the leader is magnified. If I could abdicate, it would be different. I might personally want to hold you, but not act on it in this setting.

Bill: What about outside here? You must get involved with a lot of women.

Richard: It could happen. Just as some of you could get involved after having shared such an intimate experience. But it is not so simple.

Marcia: I think you are scared of me, and everything is a rationalization.

Richard: I am a little scared of you. I am scared of that part of you that was naked in the forest and that wants to run wild and free. I love it but I am not sure I could handle it.

Bill: Aren't you man enough?

Richard: What is being a man to you, Bill?

Bill: The same as to everybody else—being virile, strong, powerful.

Richard: How would you feel if a woman took the initiative and more or less raped you?

Bill: Like a worm.

Richard: If you were more sure of yourself, you wouldn't mind. You might enjoy it.

Alan: I am still worried about Ann.

Richard: Why are you the only one who is so worried?

Penny: I'm concerned.

Richard: What did she say that bothered you so much?

Alan: It just seems to me that she must be going through hell out there and that someone should be with her. Why aren't you?

Richard: You think that I am making a mistake?

Alan: I do. I wish you wouldn't turn everything I say around. What's wrong with my being concerned for another human being?

Richard: Were you in the army?

Alan: Yes.

Richard: Did you ever do anything to any girl like Ann described?

Alan: Are you crazy!

Richard: Did you ever go to a brothel?

Alan: So what? That's what they are paid for.

Norma: I am really getting upset by all this. Can't we talk about something else?

Richard: When you were overseas, you never had occasion to attack a girl, not a white girl maybe, but a girl?

Alan: Is this an inquisition? What are you trying to prove?

Richard: You didn't answer the question.

Alan: Over there, things are different. How can you all understand?

Richard: I take it the answer is yes.

Alan: You don't understand. How can any of you understand unless you were there, surrounded by death, unsure of the next day? Yes, I had an experience once that I can recall. I suppose you won't give me any peace until I talk about it.

Richard: Do you want to? . . . Oh, there is Ann. Sit down. Good timing.

Alan: I want to get you off my back. What do you want to know?

Richard: I want to know what happened in that place that you are still carrying with you, and that Ann has unwittingly jarred loose.

Alan: You have to understand, it was a group of us. We were a team. We depended on each other. We were mopping up and we came to a cellar that seemed deserted. But we found a young girl there. It wasn't my idea.

Richard: But you took your turn.

Alan: I had to. They expected it.

Richard: The members of your squad?

Alan: Yes. I didn't want to. I tried to talk them out of it. Then they turned nasty. They began to suspect I might squeal on them. So I shut up and took my turn.

Richard: Did you enjoy it?

Alan: Honestly?

Richard: Honestly.

Alan: I was scared at first. I didn't know whether I'd be able to do anything at all. But when I got going I didn't care about anything. I just gave it everything I had. I enjoyed it, sure.

Richard: What happened when you were finished?

Alan: The line went on.

Richard: How many of you were there?

Alan: Six, counting myself.

Richard: What happened at the end, Alan?

Alan: She tried to escape and we shot her.

Richard: Did she really try to escape?

Alan: We couldn't just leave her there. But she did try to run. No one knows about this. If anyone says anything, I would deny it. Nothing could be proved. I didn't mean to say anything about it.

Richard: As far as I am concerned, it is a fantasy. I want you to talk to Ann and Norma for a little while.

Alan: All right. Do you both despise me?

Ann: I knew there was something about you I couldn't stomach.

Alan: I suppose I couldn't expect you to understand.

Ann: You pigs would be better off castrated. You should be kept in fields like bulls and used in mating season, and if not used, castrated.

Alan: I am not proud of myself.

Ann: You say that now. You say whatever people want to hear. I spit on you.

Norma: I feel so sorry for you, Alan. It was a terrible thing, but I feel such pity. I have the strangest desire to be naked now.

Alan: Don't do me any favors.

Norma: You are naked. I feel that I should be. God would understand.

Alan: Are you planning to sacrifice your virginity to make me pure?

Norma: I am doing this because I want to do it.

Alan: What was it like, Ann?

Ann: Are you curious or just morbid?

Alan: I want to know. Maybe I am a masochist.

Ann: How do you think a flower feels when it is ripped from its stem and crushed? I could say it didn't matter, that I went numb, but I was never the same. I am still numb . . . I just threw up in the toilet. I threw up just to stay alive. I threw up the unwilling passion that was created in me. I threw up the conviction that they had the right to do with us as they chose. I threw up being a slave.

It did not matter. It was happening every day. We are

all numb to statistics. But if you want the truth, if you want to touch the center, where I am still alive, then I tell you that I am still crying out for help that never comes and cursing fate that placed me in the path of such brutality.

Alan: I am truly, truly sorry. I know there is nothing that I can do. (*He begins to cry.*) There is no excuse . . . I am just so terribly sorry for the whole thing . . .

Ann: It is not your fault . . . I cannot spend my life seeking revenge on men who died long ago or have gone underground. It is another season . . . I too am sorry, Alan.

Norma: I only wish I felt old enough to say something . . . Hold me, Alan.

Alan: How can you want me to? Don't be kind.

Norma: I want you to . . .

They embrace.

Norma: I want you to let it all go. You are not a bad man. You may have done a terrible thing but you are not a bad man. I could not feel so warm toward you if you were bad.

Alan: Women love to be badly treated. They love to be pushed down.

Norma: I don't care what terrible things you say. It doesn't shock me.

Alan: I'm sorry. It is just so awfully hard for me to accept your pity and your understanding. I don't deserve it.

Richard: If any of us got what we deserved, the world would be a nightmare.

Thurston: I hope no one will be offended if I change the subject, but the heat has never gone up.

Marcia: What!

Thurston: The heat in the sauna bath. It never went up. All this time we have been sitting here and the bath hasn't been working.

Richard: I turned down the thermostat when I came in.

Thurston: But why?

Richard: Who can talk at 190 degrees?

John: I have a fantasy. I see Alan lying on the floor. Ann stands over him. She has a whip. She beats him with it and laughs wildly. Then Norma comes and binds up his wounds. Then Ann begins again. Then Norma.

Richard: And then?

John: Then Alan gets up looking wonderful.

Thurston: I wonder what my wife would say about all this?

John: What do *you* say?

Thurston: I am somewhat stunned. I feel like I am descending into an active volcano . . .

Bill: I have been the butt of a lot of hostility. Everybody seems to feel that I am some kind of creep.

Ann: You are a little boy with a dirty mind.

Bill: How do you know that?

Ann: What you need is a night with a real woman. Maybe after that you would be more secure?

Bill: Is that an offer?

Ann: I am not a good woman. Would I appeal to you after what you have heard?

Bill: I wouldn't mind.

Ann: In fact it might help. Well, no thanks. You will have to work it out on your own.

Marcia: I don't want to sleep alone tonight. I was alone last night.

Bill: Well, I'm willing.

Marcia: I don't want to sleep with a man. I want everyone to sleep all together in a big heap.

Penny: That sounds like fun.

Thurston: Then I could tell my wife that we all slept together. She would be impressed.

Norma: I don't know what you have in mind.

Marcia: I don't know what other people have in mind but I would like to pull a bunch of mattresses together on the floor in the big room and just all sleep there any way we want to.

Norma: But when the lights go out?

Marcia: You do what you want. I want to snuggle next to someone and get some sleep. I am very tired.

Richard: Restas, you have been very quiet for a long time.

Restas: I know. That is how I feel. I just have nothing to say.

Richard: That is hard to believe.

Restas: Something is happening to me but I can't put it into words. I have to absorb what is happening. I haven't yet. I really don't want to talk just to take up time . . .

Frank: So when does the nude encounter start?

Richard: When does it stop?

Frank: But we are just sitting around talking.

Richard: What is it you want to happen?

Frank: Oh, come on. We sit here looking at one another. Aren't we going to do something about it?

Richard: What do you want to do?

Frank: How literal do I have to be?

Marcia: Where have you been all this time, Frank?

Frank: I guess I had the wrong idea. I thought everything that was happening was just a prelude.

Marcia: To what?

Frank: It sounds stupid to say it, but to an orgy. I don't mean to sound like a maniac. If I am the only one in the group who feels that way, forget about it.

Richard: Have you ever been in an orgy, Frank?

Frank: Sure. Am I the only one?

Silence.

Frank: Well, that's different. Let's forget the whole thing.

Marcia: What was it like?

Frank: There is one way to find out!

Marcia: I didn't come here for that. I wish you would answer my question.

Frank: I wouldn't want to do it every day. Once a year maybe. I feel peculiar when I see those people in other places. I don't know what to say.

Sheila: Maybe there is something wrong with me, but I am fed up with sex, sex, sex. Who cares! I mean we sit here naked. O.K., at first it is strange and different, embarrassing, interesting. But after a while you forget it. Why do we have to go on and on?

Richard: What do you want to do?

Sheila: How about turning up the thermostat and having a sauna bath? We could certainly all use it.

Marcia: Not just yet. Something has just struck me. It is going to sound corny, like some half-baked psychoanalytic interpretation. I was looking at Richard. He doesn't look like my father, but I guess he is the father image in the group. Anyway I just remembered seeing my father naked when I was about seven years old. And I began to get excited. I can recall the feeling so vividly, the excitement, and then the alarm. I knew it wasn't right. If I had any doubt, my mother removed it when she yelled at him to stop showing himself in front of me. And everytime I had that feeling, I got caught in the same bind. It was forbidden. I don't know if you believe me or are interested but it is a great relief to realize it.

Richard: That you wanted to fuck your father?

Marcia: Yes.

Richard: Like any normal, healthy red-blooded American girl.

Marcia: Yes. It is so wonderful of you to say it. Can I kiss you?

Richard: Absolutely . . . but I am not your father . . .

They kiss.

Bill: I feel like shit.

Ann: You should.

Bill: Thanks a lot. But I really do.

Penny: You should.

Bill: Do all you people really hate me?

Frank: Grow up.

Bill: Who are you to talk? . . . I just feel so small.

Ann: Maybe there is hope for you yet.

Bill: I was always the one the kids made fun of.

Sheila: Are you asking us to feel sorry for you?

Bill: I just want a little respect. I am sick of being treated like an idiot cousin who has to be tolerated.

Sheila: But that is the way you act.

Bill: What the hell is wrong in being interested in women's bodies?

Marcia: There is nothing wrong. There is nothing at all wrong. We make it wrong. We coat it with slime. You are doing it, Bill. You turn it into something shameful. You don't have to.

Bill: But it is, isn't it? I mean if I were really good I wouldn't have these thoughts.

Norma: You mean if you were really good you would be like me?

Bill: I suppose.

Norma: But I have thoughts. I have been wondering how it would be with Alan.

Alan: Sheila was right.

Norma: About what?

Alan: She warned me about you.

John: Why don't you stop trying so hard, Bill? It will take care of itself. There's nothing wrong with you.

Bill: Maybe there is something wrong with me. I just never wanted to think about it. Maybe I'm a pervert.

Richard: What do you mean?

Bill: Maybe I would rather look at pictures. I really don't like myself very much. I can understand why you don't like me. I just want you all to be pictures.

Penny: For some reason I am suddenly beginning to feel sympathy for you, Bill. I want to put your head on my lap and stroke your hair and tell you, "There, there, it will be all right." I suppose you wouldn't let me, would you?

Bill: Are you serious?

Penny: Of course.

Bill: All right. I'm not proud . . .

Richard: Thurston, would you turn up the thermostat? As the heat goes up, I want to do an exercise. We are all more or less poisoned by what has been expressed. We need to be purified before we sleep or we will take all this with us to bed.

Everyone get comfortable. Lie on a towel if there is room. It is going to get quite hot as I talk. I want you to focus your attention on the heat. Experience it as fully as possible. How many different kinds of heat are there? Do you sense the heat in the air, in your skin, in your blood? Do you feel the heat where you contact some external surface? . . .

You are bathing in this heat. It is going to bake you. It is going to make you sweat. It is going to help you purify and burn up all the poisons that you have absorbed. When you breathe the hot air in, it will burn up your wastes. When you breathe out, the hot air will carry away the poison you put into it.

Everyone around you is being heated. Everyone is being purified. You have taken into yourself everything that has been expressed. You must let it go. They have taken into themselves everything you have expressed. They must let it go. The hot air will carry it all. It will burn it all. You and they will be left pure and free. You and they will become clean.

You are getting younger. You can feel the weight of years, the inertia of memories, the dead hand of fear all slipping from you. The heat brings back courage. It brings back youth.

You can face everything again as it was on the first morning—untouched, unknown, miraculous, and normal.

Even my voice will be burned so that the words begin to curl and smolder. They burn as they leave my mouth and enter into you. The meaning goes up in smoke, but the fire enters you and burns away all the thoughts that have been burdening your mind. There is nothing left. It has all been purified . . . Lie here as long as you want to—burning. Then take a cold shower . . . and finally go to sleep.

# Sunday morning

Marcia: Did I have a great sleep!

Thurston: I didn't think I would make it from the shower to my bed last night.

Richard: It is Sunday morning.

Sheila: Is that supposed to mean something?

Ann: Where is Norma?

Marcia: Where is John?

Frank: Where is Restas?

Penny: Who cares? It is good to be alive.

Sheila: Is there anything left to do?

Bill: I had a crazy dream. I don't suppose anyone wants to hear about it?

Ann: I am fed up with confessions. We know enough about you.

John: I wouldn't mind listening later, but not right now. I want to enjoy this moment before it vanishes.

Richard: Why must it vanish? We are not that much at its mercy. Suppose that instead of savoring the peacefulness we build something on it.

Penny: Such as?

Richard: A dance.

John: What kind of dance?

Thurston: I can't dance.

Richard: I don't mean a rehearsed dance or anything you could be taught. I mean spontaneous moving—each person doing what they want to do, alone, in pairs, the total group, whatever evolves, but in the spirit of the morning.

Penny: It sounds like fun, but how do we get into it.

Richard: A step at a time. Do you want to try?

Thurston: I can't dance.

Marcia: You'll probably be the best.

Thurston: I don't want anyone to laugh at me.

Richard: There is nothing to be afraid of. First of all, everyone find a place in the room that they feel like occupying . . . Stand there and just sense what it feels like . . . Take a few seconds and explore the space where you are . . . Reach out into it . . . Stretch . . . Pick up the objects that may be there . . . Discover their weight, texture, odor . . .

Thurston: This is dancing?

Richard: When you are finished exploring, settle back into yourself . . . Try to discover how you are feeling . . . Let your awareness grow more intense . . . Let it grow until something inside you wants to give physical expression to it . . . If you don't force it, the movement which comes will be effortless . . . It will be a relief . . . That's right . . . Forget completely what you look like . . . Ignore other people for the moment . . . Focus on yourself. Express what is inside . . . Don't push it beyond its own limitation . . . When the feeling is gone, stop expressing it . . . Don't get caught in the movement itself . . . You are improvising melodies with your body . . . Pause if you need to . . . The most important thing is the preparation . . . If you wait until something is happening inside you, the movement will be natural . . . If you force it or fit it into a pattern of movement you have learned, it will be a hollow expression . . .

Experiment this way . . . Remember space has three dimensions, backwards, forwards, to either side and up and down . . . Use more of space . . . Become bolder . . . Let the space around you expand as your need expands. Let it contract as your need to express contracts . . . Become the living center of space through which you flow . . . Become the flow . . . That is good.

In a short time you are going to move out of your space which is private . . . into the larger room which is public. You will pass through the space which others have been using . . . You can move more freely . . . but you must be aware that you are moving through different countries, each with its own character . . . determined by its position and the person who has been occupying it . . . Be sensitive to the differences . . . Move as slowly as you want . . . Forget how you look . . . Use your body to express what is inside you, or the reaction which you have to the environment around you . . . When you have done enough, come to rest . . .

Put your attention on yourself as you are, sitting, standing or lying down . . . Become aware of your breathing, the beating of your heart, your body heat . . . Extend your awareness to those around you . . . Extend it into the morning of which you are a part . . . In a little while we are going to try to express what we feel about being together . . . What we have been through . . . How we feel about ourselves, each other, the sun outside, the blue sky and the time and space which we can share . . . How we feel about lies and the truth . . . The chance to begin again . . . The opportunity to purge hidden sorrows . . . All these things and more which only you can know are going to be expressed . . . But when you begin, I

want you to put your attention not in yourself, but in the group
. . . Try to keep a sense of the quiet point around which everyone moves and from which every action originates. The location
of this point will shift as you move, but it will always be there
. . . Try to find it now as I talk. Let everything including my
voice come from that place. If you find it, then you will be
related to everyone present without effort. Keep your attention
on that moving point, like a ballet dancer focuses on a fixed point
when twirling. It will uphold you and guide you. Your body can
move by itself . . . Allow yourself complete freedom . . . Have
you found the central point? . . . If you have, try to experience
yourself as coming from there, and everyone else as coming
from there . . . Your breathing comes from there. Your thoughts
come from there. As soon as you are ready, begin to move . . . I
am going to establish a rhythm with my hands. Use the rhythm
as a guide but concentrate on the central place . . . If you lose
it, come back to it. You are no longer alone. Everything you do
will affect others. Be sensitive. Be free. Begin!

For fifteen minutes the room is transformed into a setting for
a gentle, wild, chaotic, strangely ordered set of movements, rising and falling in waves. The rhythm varies from one of quiet
monotony through a strongly martial one, to an ethereal one, and
finally to a fast and brittle rhythm.

In the beginning people function alone, avoiding one another.
Then groups begin to form, some for a few seconds, others for a
minute or two. Pairs express interplays of emotion. Some are
direct and clumsy; others, subtle and tentative.

As the time passes, uncertainty wears off, and movements take
on their own momentum. At one point the total group is involved
in an invocation which breaks up into separate acts of devotion
ranging from orthodox prayer and supplication to pagan rites.

In the end, everyone throws himself into a great pile in the middle of the floor. A few people begin to laugh. Then everyone is caught. They laugh happily, slightly hysterically, wildly and quietly. It dies down, starts up again. Slowly people begin to pull themselves apart. Thurston is on the bottom. He doesn't move.

Marcia: Are you all right, Thurston?

Thurston: I don't want to move. I am absolutely powerless. I have never been so relaxed.

Alan and Norma appear.

Alan: What did we miss?

Richard: Where have you been?

Alan: Talking.

Penny: We were dancing . . .

Sheila: I warned you, Alan.

Alan: About what?

Sheila: Norma.

Alan: But you didn't warn Norma about me.

Frank: Not that I care right now, but did you spend the night together?

Norma: I told you, Alan, there was no use trying to think of any story. Yes, we did.

Richard: I am not sure just what you are saying.

Alan: Is this really necessary? Why must you take a beautiful event and turn it into public gossip?

Frank: Why are you so defensive?

Alan: I just feel that all of you are seeing me as a monster who has taken advantage of an inexperienced girl against her better judgment.

Richard: What is the truth?

Alan: I really resent this. I didn't want to come this morning. But I knew that the longer I stayed away, the more questions I would have to answer.

Bill: We still don't know what happened.

Alan: And you are not going to. You can think what you want.

Marcia: Why do you act as if we want to destroy something that you value? Maybe we would value it. Don't be so paranoid.

Alan: I feel guilty.

Richard: What is there to hide? Your evasion only makes it seem worse.

Alan: There was nothing wrong, but I keep acting as if there were.

Richard: What do you think Sheila is thinking right now?

Alan: She is thinking, "I hope you know what you are getting into. Those noble virgins can drive you out of your mind."

Richard: How about Bill?

Alan: He is thinking, "That lucky guy. I hope he tells us all about it."

Richard: What do you think I am thinking?

Alan: I wish I knew!

Richard: Try. There is no penalty for being wrong.

Alan: If I must. You are thinking, "He is really immature. Did he believe he could clean away the effect of his war experiences through the love of a pure woman who accepted what he had done?"

Richard: Actually none of us knows precisely what happened. Perhaps you were only up talking until late. Norma hasn't said very much . . . Before either of you say any more, I want to ask each member of the group what they think really happened between the two of you.

Norma: Do we have to be made into a public spectacle?

Richard: Don't you want to know what others think? Are you indifferent to it?

Norma: I don't like being so much in the center of attention

. . . That's not really true . . . It's just that I know what happened and why. So what difference do your ideas make?

Richard: You live according to some very exacting standards,
so you don't have to worry about people. But if you have aban-
doned those standards, then it is very important to understand
yourself. Look at yourself through all these other eyes. It may
help . . .

Norma: If you think so . . .

Richard: Why don't you begin, John, and then we can go
right around the group. Try to be as specific as possible.

John: I think they slept together. Probably they were up most
of the night. Is that specific enough?

Marcia: I am really puzzled. Norma doesn't seem bothered. I
know they were together. I am sure they shared something intimate. I can see Norma sacrificing something precious for Alan's
redemption. But I think she is still a virgin.

Bill: Is there a doctor in the house? Sorry! I don't mean to be
sarcastic. I just feel envious. It must be great to be the first
one . . .

Ann: I think Norma got completely carried away. She just
can't identify her normal self with what happened. That's why
she is still so calm. But it will be like a depth charge. I don't
think she will expect Alan to marry her or anything like that, but
she will probably go paranoid and start accusing him of seducing
her. In fact she may accuse the whole group of being a perverted
set of devil worshipers.

Penny: I don't know what happened. But I feel very happy
for Norma. I feel good for Alan too, though I don't think he de-
serves it. But whatever happened, it was really beautiful that
Norma could give herself. She may end up getting hurt, but it
is worth the risk. I hope she can feel responsible for what she
has done, whatever that is, and not project it onto others.

Frank: Well, Alan, you asked for it and now you've got it. I think you were a fool. You are going to have to be grateful to Norma. Sure, she is noble, but she has you by the balls. Did you really need forgiveness that badly? I don't think the price was worth it.

Sheila: I feel like Cassandra. I kept telling you both to watch out, but I am relieved it happened this way. It could have been much worse. This way it served a purpose for each of you beyond a boy and girl coming together.

Thurston: I am much older than you. Why do I keep bringing that up? . . . In any case, I wouldn't make so much of it all. Romeo and Juliet were just two foolish kids. They didn't have to commit suicide. What I mean is, it happens all the time. Good luck to both of you. I am thankful that neither one of you is married.

Richard: I am always a little concerned when someone as rigid as Norma suddenly lets go. She has so little with which to protect herself. She may get into a panic later on. But that is general. I don't expect that to happen with her. As we talk I get the feeling that whatever happened, you two are capable of dealing with it. And my prediction is that your relation won't go further than this group, or that it doesn't have to. If you let it, that is your own affair. But you shared something unique to the occasion. In that sense I can accept it and find it good.

Alan: Do you want to know what happened?

Richard: Do you want to tell us?

Alan: Now I do. I would like to share it, if Norma is willing.

Norma: I was always willing.

Alan: After the bath Norma said she wanted to talk to me. I asked her whether she wanted to come to my room. She asked if I would come to hers . . . So I did.

Norma: You all may wonder what I had in mind. I don't know.

I just felt very, very emotional. I wanted Alan to know that I understood and that I wanted to forgive him. That may sound very presumptuous. Who am I to forgive him? Anyway he came in and I told him that I wanted to pray for him. And then he caught me off guard. He said he would let me do it but only if we were naked. I never would have agreed but we had just come from the bath. It seemed natural . . .

Alan: And then we both kneeled down and she prayed. I know it sounds corny and some of you are probably snickering, or feeling sorry for how weak I was. But I don't mind saying that I was pretty emotional myself. Nobody ever prayed over me before. I knew that she was something of a fanatic and that I was a lost soul to her credit if she could save me. But still, she was willing to be undressed, alone with me, knowing what she knew. I thought it was pretty wonderful.

Norma: Once I started I didn't dare stop. I was afraid of what might happen. I just prayed that God would forgive Alan, help him to forgive himself, and protect us from anything that shouldn't be done . . . I just prayed my heart out. I knew I was in danger. I didn't trust myself anymore. But finally I said, "Father, thy will be done. Whatever is right I will do, but let it be your will and not my fear or my desire." I just went on and on. Finally when I was done, there was a long silence . . .

Alan: I knew what should happen. It scared me but I felt I had to say it. I asked Norma to stay with me all night. She said she would. I said I wanted her to lie next to me all night, as she was. I told her that nothing would happen unless she wanted it to. She said that she would, if I would leave her alone. She would trust me if I would give my word.

Norma: I didn't know what to think. I knew that I was being a fool. But if he didn't keep his word then, I would know that the whole thing was false. Nothing truly held me back, so I went.

Alan: We held each other all night. That was all. Today I feel like a different human being. I will be grateful to this little fanatic until the day I die.

Marcia: That is very, very beautiful . . .

Ann: I feel this tremendous feeling of relief, as if I had been holding my breath for five minutes. I don't know why. What difference does it all make? But I am so happy that that was how it was . . .

Richard: There is nothing wrong with a few tears.

Ann: I know, I know.

Bill: Boy, it sure is a crazy world. That sounds like something that would have happened to me . . .

Restas: Have I missed anything?

Frank: Where the hell have you been?

Restas: Walking. I am feeling very restless.

Ann: What is wrong with you, anyway? You have been like a ghost haunting the group. I thought you were going to be a real good member when we started. But you sure have faded out.

Restas: I am troubled.

Penny: But you don't share it.

Restas: I come from a different world. I know that what you are doing has meaning for you, but it only alienates me. I want to be left alone. The woods are fine for walking. I enjoy that and benefit from it. Your feelings should not be hurt. I am glad to have come and had the chance to be by myself.

Marcia: But we miss you. We want to know you and share something together.

Restas: Must everything be shared?

Richard: No, but it ought to be tested. You, in the magic circle of your own experience, can never be sure if it is fact or fantasy. You may gain from private meditation, but you cannot escape yourself.

Marcia: I don't know about the rest of the people. I just would like to see you share something with someone, with me.

Restas: Why should I if I don't want to? I have no problems with women.

Marcia: Does it have to be a problem? Couldn't it be for the fun of it? Couldn't it be a mystery rather than a pathology?

Restas: I really don't want to hurt your feelings. I just don't want to have an encounter with you.

Marcia: Then what did you come for?

Restas: Does it really matter? That seems a long time ago. Can't I sit here quietly and be left alone?

Richard: My suggestion is that Restas take his chair over to the window and sit there looking out until he wants to turn around and join the group.

Restas: I would be delighted . . .

Bill: In one of the magazine articles I read about encounter groups, they showed everybody massaging everyone. We haven't done anything like that.

Frank: Do we have to do it, just because you read about it?

Bill: What do you want to do?

Frank: I suppose I just want to relax.

Richard: Perhaps we can do both things at the same time. Why don't you each pick partners?

Bill: Men and women together?

Richard: However you want . . . One person lie down on the floor on his stomach. The other is going to give artificial respiration, the old way, by pressing on the back . . . What you are trying to do is help the person to let go and breathe more deeply. You have to sense through your hands when they are breathing and how they are breathing. When they start to exhale, press down with increasing weight so that all the air is squeezed out of their lungs. Then ease up so that they can breathe back in. If you do it right, they will breathe more fully.

The person being worked on is going to have to keep letting go, not only of his breath but also all his tensions. Just let your breath carry them all away. It may help you to groan and hum as your breath goes out . . . Try that for a few minutes. If anything hurts you, or if it is too gentle, let your partner know. You don't have to suffer in silence . . .

The artificial respiration begins quietly. A few couples whisper to each other.

Richard: No talking. Stay with the activity. Those of you who are being worked on, feel the oxygen in your system. Sense what it does to you. Allow it to reach you . . . Keep it up for another minute or two and then stop. Let the person on the rug stay there and when he is ready, reverse positions.

The room is silent except for breathing. Restas has turned around to watch. He takes out a cigarette and observes with a speculative expression. Forest sounds filter through the windows. A sudden breeze passes through the room.

Richard: Try to observe what you are thinking. In a minute or two, when you are finished you can share these thoughts . . . Do you feel any different than before?

Penny: I feel real good. Let's do some more.

Bill: I feel worse. Ann made me feel like I was a patient on an operating table.

Ann: You made me feel like a whore.

Richard: You two were made for each other. Do you want to do something else along this line?

Marcia: I would like to close my eyes and have different people come up to me and touch me. I would like to try to guess who it was.

Bill: What is the point?

Marcia: Do you have anything against it?

Bill: It seems like a kid's game.

Marcia: That's what I want to do. And that is what I am going to do! So I am closing my eyes and waiting . . .

Frank approaches her from the back, places his hands around her stomach and squeezes. She goes limp and hangs on his arms. Then he lets go and she sinks to the ground.

Marcia: I am puzzled. It felt like a man, but it might have been Ann. I don't think so though. It wouldn't be Bill. He wouldn't be the first. I really don't know. Maybe it was Frank . . . Are you going to tell me?

No answer.

Ann approaches directly from the front. She slaps Marcia moderately hard. Marcia struggles to avoid opening her eyes.

Marcia: I can feel that you are still there. Why are you keeping me in suspense?

Richard: No talking.

Marcia: Well, at least I know it isn't Richard.

Ann puts her hands on Marcia's shoulders and begins shaking her. Then she suddenly shoves her to the side and walks away.

Marcia: I didn't know I had any enemies. I should never have shut my eyes. Maybe that was Bill. I must have irritated him. But I didn't think he would waste the opportunity. I am at his mercy. It might have been Richard, only I know it wasn't. I don't know, but it must have been a man. That's as close as I can get.

Richard: I want to make clear that we are not trying to trick you. Each person should do just what he feels. This isn't a guessing game.

John approaches Marcia, bends over, slings her over his shoulder and carries her all around the room. Then he carefully puts her on the ground. He looks at her for a moment and then quickly kisses her on the lips.

Marcia: That was John.

Penny comes over with a comb in her hand. She stands diagonally back of Marcia and begins to comb her hair. She works on it slowly, until the tangles have been removed and it is completely loose.

Marcia: Was that Norma? No, I don't think so. It was too businesslike, warm but professional. I think either Sheila or Penny.

Bill walks slowly over to her. He stands about eighteen inches in front of her without moving. He looks her over from top to bottom.

Marcia: The suspense is killing me.

Bill looks around at the rest of the group. Then he looks at Marcia and begins to smile in a peculiar way.

Restas: Stop him!

Bill suddenly attacks Marcia. He rips at her blouse and throws her to the ground. Marcia is momentarily caught off guard. Then she opens her eyes, sees who it is and begins to fight.

Restas: Somebody stop him!

Richard: Leave them alone. If she needs help she will ask for it.

Bill tries to pin Marcia to the floor so that he can get to her. She thrashes and beats him with her fists. He pins one arm. With the other she grabs his hair. He slaps her.

Ann: For God sakes, Richard, do something.

Richard: If you want to do something, do it. Don't tell me.

Ann jumps on Bill. She pulls. She pounds on his back. He ignores her and throws her off. She grabs him around the neck in a hammer lock.

Ann: God damn you! Get off her!

Bill is in pain. He turns toward Ann, seeking to free his throat and get a grip so that he can push her away. Marcia begins to fight from underneath. At first she struggles to escape. But then she joins Ann. They attack from different sides. Bill grabs them both and squeezes, but they scratch him. Marcia's blouse is partially torn. Bill's cheek is cut. He looks from one to the other, shrugs his shoulders, curses under his breath and goes back to his seat.

Richard: Is everyone all right?

No response.

Richard: What made you call out to stop him, Restas?

Restas: I have worked in a mental hospital as an orderly. I have seen the expression of a man about to go off the deep end.

Frank: But you didn't do anything.

Restas: I warned you. Then it was your responsibility. It is your group, not mine.

Richard: I ask again, is everyone all right?

Marcia: I am really furious. I feel abused. What kind of an animal is he?

Bill: What kind of an animal are you?

Ann: You are lucky that your back was to me. I would really have hurt you.

Marcia: In all honesty, there is one thing I must say. I respect you more, Bill. It was exciting.

Thurston: What did you experience? Did you go off the deep end like Restas said?

Bill: I stood there looking. I felt your eyes on me. I felt you thinking, "He'll never do anything. He will think about it and dream about it, but never do anything." And suddenly I knew that I had to, that my whole future depended on it. I suppose I felt safe in a way. You could protect her. But you could hurt me. I didn't care. I am shaking now. I want to cry like a little boy . . . But I don't feel like a little boy, I feel grim. I feel older. I am not a snotty kid. Something was let loose in me. You better watch out.

Ann: I understand. You had to do it. I don't feel sorry for Marcia, though you would think I would. She left herself open to it. She took the chance. When I slapped her, that must have set the stage for you.

Marcia: That was you? Why?

Ann: You made me angry calling me a man.

Marcia: I was scared. I'm still scared. But I feel strong. Don't get me wrong. I don't like Bill. I don't want him near me. But he is out in the open. A long time ago—it must have been yesterday —I wanted to feel like a big black bear prowling the forest. Now I really feel like an animal. I was attacked. I defended myself. I don't know what would have happened without Ann.

Richard: What do you think?

Marcia: I am not sure about myself. Maybe I wanted to be overcome. So much has happened to me, but it hasn't led to any great climax. That might have been it.

Alan: Right here in front of everyone?

Marcia: Yes. I wouldn't have been responsible.

Richard: A convenient fiction.

Marcia: True. What kind of a pervert am I?

Richard: You have depths.

Marcia: Do you think I am rotten?

John: No. I think you are great. What scared me is that I might stop running and go over to you. Alan and Norma may never meet again after this group. But I may see you, whether I want to or not. I don't want to, I wish we had never met. But I can't just turn my back.

Richard: Why don't you two talk in the center of the circle?

John: I guess I have said what I wanted to say.

Marcia: I like you very much. You know that. Right now

though, I feel distant. I am still worked up. My heart is beating. Something in me is ready to start fighting again, though my muscles are aching. What do you want from me, John?

John: I want to avoid you.

Marcia: So do it.

John: I can't. I need something you have. If I walk away from you, I desert part of myself.

Marcia: You have a problem.

John: You're not making it easy.

Marcia: Look, John, if you want to talk to me you are going to have to get where I am. Otherwise it is a waste of time.

John: This wasn't my idea. Oh, to hell with it. I have to come to terms with the thing. I think I could fall in love with you. (*pause*) No response?

Marcia: Yesterday or tomorrow I would say wonderful. But right now I am not too interested. What else do you have to say?

John: I don't have anything to say. I didn't want to do this. I think it is a stinking idea.

Marcia: You don't like not being able to run?

John: I am afraid of being involved.

Marcia: So keep on running. But if you want me, you are going to have to do better than that.

John: I know what I have to do.

Marcia: What do you have to do, John?

John: Give you the flame.

Marcia: It took you long enough to realize it . . . But how do you know that I want to take it?

John: I don't know. I don't know. That is your decision.

Richard: Do you want to give it to her now?

John: I don't want to do any of this, but this moment is as good as any.

Richard: How do you do it?

John: I don't know that either. I have been running so long, protecting it from others who wanted to steal it or destroy it. This whole thing could become a mockery so easily. It sounds like I'm a pretentious kid using big words. Maybe it is all an illusion.

Marcia: If you believe that, I'll hate you.

John: I don't believe it, but I feel more and more stupid, like a man protecting a treasure that turns out never to have existed. What can I do? What do you think I should do, Norma?

Norma: If you have it, you should share it. She is willing and you need to do it.

John: It would be easier if we were alone.

Richard: Maybe it would be, but if it is real it will survive the group.

John: All right. I don't know. I have an idea. Sit down, Marcia . . . No, not over there. Sit on my lap. I will cross my legs. You sit on them and cross your legs behind me. Put your arms around my neck and lean back.

Restas: You look like a Tibetan statue.

Marcia: Now what do I do?

John: We look at each other and wait. If you want to come closer, do it, but otherwise, wait, and remain receptive. Try to be as open as you can . . . It may help if you feel your breath and mine together. Try to feel that we are one person . . . I am not sure . . . I will have to depend on you to know something.

Marcia: I will really try.

They sit staring at each other for five minutes. They sway slightly together. Then their faces come together with tongues extending, until they touch. Another minute passes . . .

Marcia: Is it finished?

John: Yes. You can get up.

Marcia: I don't know what to say.

John: Don't say anything. Let Restas do the talking.

Restas: Why do you say that?

John: Because I think you have something to say.

Restas: One thing that has been putting me off is that all you people are going crazy together. My experience among crazy people is to act like a professional. As I said, I was an orderly in a hospital at one time. But I can't act like that here. So I stay away . . . But you are right. It is getting to me. I don't know what to think. For instance, if someone were to ask me truthfully what I thought about what just happened, I would have to say that I don't know. I think something really happened. But how can I be sure? How can anyone be sure?

John: Why must you be sure?

Restas: If it was real, then I must redefine the situation for myself.

Marcia: What would you do that you haven't done?

Restas: I would allow myself to get involved.

Marcia: But why pick this strange crazy thing to shake you up?

Restas: It had meaning to me. I have read an account of a ceremony a good deal like this. John seems to know nothing about it.

John: About what?

Restas: It has to do with Mahayana Buddhism.

John: No. I don't know anything about Eastern religions. What was it?

Restas: You have never seen the Tibetan Yab Yum figure?

John: No. I don't know what you are talking about.

Restas: All right. I believe you.

Richard: Now what, Restas?

Restas: What is your role in all this?

Richard: How do you mean?

Restas: Part of it is obvious. You keep things moving. You open doors.

Richard: Isn't that enough?

Restas: No. There is something I don't understand. Who are you?

Richard: Why does it matter?

Restas: I have to know whether I can trust you.

Richard: Are you about to reveal something secret?

Restas: No.

Richard: I didn't think so. Then what is the importance of understanding me?

Restas: How did you interpret what happened?

Richard: I thought it was real.

Restas: You wanted it to happen?

Richard: I didn't know what to expect. Something needed to happen. Do you think I have a master plan?

Restas: That is it. I don't know what to think. I have seen some very clever men in my time. They could get people to do almost anything they wanted and the people concerned never knew that their actions were not self-initiated.

Richard: You think I have everyone hypnotized or brainwashed?

Restas: I would like to think so.

Richard: Have you ever been hypnotized?

Restas: No.

Richard: What are you afraid of?

Restas: Nothing.

Richard: What do you have to hide?

Restas: I am not hiding anything.

Richard: This may seem irreverent, but do you take any drugs for nonmedical purposes?

Restas: Let me answer that hypothetically. Taking drugs is

against the law. I do not break the law. However, if you ask the question whether I know anyone like myself who has taken drugs, the answer is yes.

Richard: I see. Which ones has this person taken?

Restas: Originally he became mildly hooked on morphine after a painful injury, but he shook that off. In more recent years he has tried a number of psychedelics. He has experimented with a number of combinations.

Richard: This friend of yours, would he take drugs on a week-end such as this one?

Restas: He might.

Richard: Can you be more definite?

Restas: I would say yes, he would.

Richard: That explains a good deal. Would he be taking any now?

Restas: No, he decided he had been making a mistake.

Richard: Why?

Restas: He couldn't function in this group.

Richard: But he will go on using them after he leaves?

Restas: Of course.

Richard: Why?

Restas: Why not?

Richard: That isn't good enough. What does he get from them?

Restas: Well, if you don't know, it is going to be hard for me to explain it to you.

Richard: Try.

Restas: Are you kidding me—someone in this kind of work? You must know all about these things. You must have been on LSD sometime. You're putting me on.

Richard: I'll let that go for the moment. I am asking you what you get from drugs. Why do you do it?

Restas: I get an experience.

Richard: What kind of experience?

Restas: Different kinds: peace, excitement, inspiration, visions, and sometimes nightmares. It's the same kind of thing you seem to be interested in developing. I take drugs to learn about myself. Sometimes I take them for kicks . . . I get the feeling by your expression that you don't approve.

Richard: My own attitude can wait. I want to understand yours first.

Frank: I don't think we are getting anywhere. I don't want to sit here and listen to the two of you talk.

Richard: What do you suggest?

Frank: We could tell Restas what we think of him, or he could give us a short lecture on why we should take drugs, or maybe we could try an experiment if he has some stuff with him.

Marcia: Would you allow drugs in the group?

Richard: I don't want to answer that just yet. Why don't we give Restas the platform as you suggest? Let him give a talk on the drug experience, if he wants to. Are you willing?

Restas: I don't mind.

Richard: Anybody against it?

Bill: If I get bored, I'll let you know.

Richard: Then step up in front of us, Restas, and let's hear what you have to say.

Restas: The main thing I want to emphasize is that you ought to have an open mind. People are either totally against drugs or they view them as a way of life. All I ask is that you suspend your judgment.

If you found something that made life more enjoyable, exciting, and meaningful, would you say that it was worthwhile? If you found something that could smooth away tensions and bring you back to yourself, would you pursue it? If you came upon something that could open new vistas of experience, would you be interested in it? Drugs can do all those things.

I don't want to over-simplify. There are many reasons why the use of drugs is so widespread today, particularly among the kids. I don't say it is all good. Everything can be abused. But because it is abused doesn't mean it is bad. Penicillin is a blessing, but it can make people sick if over-used, or if the individual is sensitive to it.

Society's attitude toward drug use is sick. It makes the user a criminal and puts him at the mercy of criminals who supply him. Society is sick in many ways. It turns people off. You all know that. We are not trained to be loving, creative, and self-fulfilling. Our families turn us off, our schools turn us off, our churches turn us off. But drugs turn people on. They are simple and immediate. They can be used by all. They are democratic.

I don't say that they are the answer to everything. But they are important catalyzers of human experience. How will we ever learn to use them more effectively if we don't experience their effects? Each individual is his own investigator. Each individual is his own experiment.

We live in a sick world. We are alienated from each other. Drugs can bring people back to themselves and back to one another. That is all I want to say.

Richard: Are you open to questions?

Restas: Yes.

Sheila: What have drugs done for you?

Restas: You mean for my friend. I think I have already answered that question.

Sheila: Why did you take something while you were here? I am sorry, I mean why did "he" take something?

Restas: He felt that it would help him communicate with others.

Sheila: But it didn't work.

Restas: It made him too sensitive to every nuance. He was too exposed. He had to keep away to protect himself.

Thurston: Is there anything wrong with taking drugs from your viewpoint?

Restas: Speaking personally, no. There are dangers, as there are with any agents that are powerful. But with care and experimentation these can be minimized. No, there are no real dangers if used responsibly. The worst dangers are those created by the insanity of society.

Richard: Any other questions?

Silence.

Richard: Do you want to know how we feel about you, Restas?

Restas: Not particularly, but if you want to tell me, I will listen.

Richard: Will you tell him?

Penny: I don't know about anyone else. What I want to say is that I am glad the mystery is solved. Now I understand him better and I don't feel so anxious about what he is going through. He seems like an interesting person to me.

Frank: I think he is a coward. Everything he says is a huge self-deception. People who use drugs go one way—down. I don't care how it seems at the time. If you know them over six months, the trend is very clear.

I feel sorry for you, Restas. You seem like a strong man. You have probably been through a lot of different experiences in your life. But somewhere underneath all that must be a vital flaw. And I just feel sure that if you continue, the flaw will grow and one day there will be a small earthquake and you will crack.

Bill: I have heard that sex is much more intense under drugs. I would like to know more about that.

Richard: What do you think of Restas?

Bill: He seems like an interesting man. I want to know him better to find out some of his experiences.

Marcia: I don't think Restas is a man. He looks like a man. He acts like a man, but there is something wrong. I can't put my finger on it. He says he intensifies experience. I am sure he does, but the price is too great . . . or maybe it is not great enough. I may be old-fashioned, but I am always uneasy if I receive what I haven't paid for. Drugs are too magical. I think they are surrounded with self-deception. They are a dead end. They take you into a strange forest and then they leave you there. Restas may be fascinated by the journey, but what good is it if in the end he gets lost?

Ann: I can understand Restas. I know what it feels like to have a half-conscious throbbing pain in the background of your experience. It is such a relief if the pain can be eliminated, not because it is so great, but because it is always there. I don't care about his reasons. I know why he is willing to pay the price. I don't blame him. Some of it is window dressing, of course. But everyone deceives himself. All of us here do it. If there is a way to dull or stop the pain without paying too great a price, it is worth it. If it works for him, I am for it.

Richard: How about for yourself?

Ann: I was always scared it might make things worse for me. I am not very curious about myself. Restas is.

Norma: I suppose everyone expects me to say that drug taking is a sin. Well, I think it is. I have read articles in the paper about how kids use drugs as part of religious services or to stimulate some kind of cosmic experience. But I just think it is wrong. I think it makes people forget who they are. It's like alcohol. They do things they wouldn't ordinarily do, get into fights, or hurt themselves.

That is what I think, but I just don't know. I don't feel so dogmatic anymore. I just wish Restas could feel closer to us and we to him. But the drugs are between us. I don't like it.

Thurston: I pass.

Richard: Why?

Thurston: I don't really understand. I know how the kids are using drugs. It gets to them earlier and earlier. I used to think it was just an evil. But it keeps going and going. My own son! Maybe there is something to it. Maybe *I* am wrong; my whole generation. I am not so sure. Maybe we have done it to them. Or maybe we have raised a generation of cowards. Or maybe they are alive to things we didn't know existed. I don't know. I don't want to judge. But I would like to understand.

John: I get the feeling that everything we are saying is bouncing off a glass wall you keep in front of you, Restas. My reaction is "Why bother? He isn't really listening." But for the group and for myself I feel that I should say something. I ran. You take dope. Ann hides. Bill looks at dirty pictures.

Bill: Who said I look at dirty pictures?

John: Don't you?

Silence.

John: It is all the same. All of us are weak. We have flaws. The danger exists not in having weaknesses, but in denying them, in pretending they are superiorities. If there is something wrong, it can be worked on. It can be healed. But as long as nothing is wrong, nothing can be corrected.

Here you are with a group of people, crazy maybe, but intent on helping one another in some real way, and you shut us out. You put a bulletproof wall between yourself and us. You deny before we have spoken that anything can affect you. You must be terrified inside to do that. I don't say that to condemn you. I say it as someone who is just beginning to recover from being perpetually out of breath, someone who is standing naked, trembling and uncertain. Don't shut us out, Restas. We want you to come back into your own life. We want you to abandon the swamp and the wilderness. Just because it is different doesn't mean it is better. I want you to stretch out your hand to us and to join us for the first time . . .

Richard: Anyone else? . . . Then I have to say something. I agree with various things that have been said. I don't want to repeat them. I do want to underline what John said, however. I hope that whatever happens you will come into the group and discover what awaits you there.

But I want to say something about drugs. The human mechanism is still a great mystery. Those who spend their lives studying it become increasingly aware of this fact.

When you take a drug you introduce the unknown into your system. You push levers that would not normally be pushed at that time, send strange messages and initiate reactions that do not relate to the outer situation. Is it good or is it bad? I cannot answer that question in the abstract. Certainly the medical use of drugs requires little justification. The study of the effects of drugs is a legitimate scientific enterprise. But drug users are not scientists. They are human beings trying to live as best they can, trying to find a way out of an unsatisfactory existence.

There are many ways out. Most of them are dead ends. Some of them terminate at the edge of a cliff. If you come there at night you are out of luck. Some end in the wilderness. Some circle around and return the individual to his point of departure.

I can't say whether drugs are good or bad in the abstract. It depends on who uses them. This may sound harsh, but most people are not really interested in growing. It is too difficult. It requires consistent purpose, renewed effort, willingness to suffer the unknown, and a burning motivation. For most people who are not really going anywhere except to their grave, it doesn't matter a great deal. The use of drugs is a simple practical question. If drugs hurt their social adjustment, then they are bad. If they don't, they may be all right or good. But like any powerful experience, there is danger. The greatest danger is self-deception. The drug user is drawn into a world where the possibility of contradiction and questioning is progressively eliminated. If society could be more tolerant we could learn to live with drugs like we live with alcohol. There would be abuses, but the world would not halt because people took drugs to make their lives more peaceful, or their subjective experiences more varied.

But I am not really concerned about or interested in people who want to get by and make do. They are the faceless majority. In every culture there is also a minority, the living creative edge who want to grow. Their lives are devoted to fulfilling their innate capacities.

Most institutions are designed to develop and enrich the lives of its members, but in fact they do this only to a limited degree. People grow by their own efforts. They grow by facing what is difficult, and following the path that has been given to them, wherever it leads. But all this is symbolic.

Everything basic has a physical aspect. The body is the house of fulfillment. Growth is through the body and in the body, no matter how unaware of it we may become. There are functions of the physical organism of which we are generally unaware. There are delicate mechanisms which can develop over time, given the right conditions. But I am losing the thread.

The purpose of life is to learn, to experience and develop and control your own capacities—intellectual, emotional, sensory, spiritual . . . If you cannot experience and you cannot control, you cannot help anyone else. Efforts to help other people are either misguided or, if successful, they exact too high a price on the person helping. Drugs short-circuit the process. They overload the circuit, force growth, activate mechanisms that were not meant to be activated until a later time. In short, they fuck up the internal mechanism. To the ordinary person this doesn't make too much difference, because their mechanism is in pretty sad condition to begin with. It is rusty from disuse, over-specialized, and generally abused. It is like an untended garden in which no flowers other than weeds can grow.

But if a person becomes a gardener, then he must be much more careful. He begins to have something to lose. This is exactly the situation in which the individual finds himself when he begins to work on himself as he would work on a creative product. This, for me, is the highest task a person can perform, to make his whole life a creative, integrated expression. And for someone moving in this direction, drugs are poison. Not only are they deadly to him directly, injuring delicate mechanisms and burning up in a few moments vital energies that may take months to accumulate but, as he progresses, even contact with persons taking drugs can make him sick.

Encounter groups are created for the kind of person I have just described. We are all of us crazy in one way or another. There is nothing remarkable about that. What is remarkable is that some persons can devote their lives to creating a higher order from the casual chaos by which they are surrounded. I have said much more than I intended. I could have been more direct, but this is the way it came out.

Restas: Am I to respond to all this?

Richard: I think that people most hoped you would listen. You don't have to defend yourself, unless you want to. How are you feeling?

Restas: I feel like I am frozen in a block of ice. I was reading in a magazine about this organization that freezes people as soon as they die in the hope that science will discover how to revive them. That is how I feel. It is so cold that I do not sense it as cold. But I know that every molecule of my being has almost stopped. I don't know how I can still talk.

Thurston: I know what you are feeling. Is there any way we could warm you up?

Restas: I am terribly afraid of unfreezing. I don't know what damage has been done. I might be feeble-minded.

Ann: You might be impotent.

Restas: What can I do? I am a disembodied voice in a body of ice. I am afraid of the pain when the circulation starts in my frostbitten limbs.

Richard: What you need are drugs to keep you from feeling.

Restas: Don't joke with me. What can I do?

Richard: You have to make a choice. Do you want to be thawed out?

Restas: Can I be frozen again if it is too terrible?

Richard: It might be possible but the likelihood of damage would be greater the second time. Do you want to be warmed or not?

Restas: I DON'T KNOW!

Richard: Let us know when you make up your mind.

Restas: You are just going to leave me here?

Richard: What am I supposed to do? You have to decide.

Restas: How can I decide when I don't know what would happen?

Richard: I don't know what would happen either. I have enough trouble deciding for myself. I can't do it for you too.

Thurston: Can you just turn away from him like that? He is in a very bad way.

Richard: I am not turning you away, just myself. Do what you want.

Thurston: I don't know what to suggest, but perhaps some sort of fantasy. Do you remember when I saw the melting iceberg? That seemed to help.

Restas: Leave me alone. All of you. I don't want your help. I don't want anything from any of you. I must have been out of my mind to come here. You bunch of amateur head-shrinkers. You don't know what you are doing. It is terribly dangerous. Do people ever commit suicide?

Richard: Are you volunteering?

Restas: You get your kicks from watching people suffer. You must be very dead inside.

Richard: I am really enjoying watching you suffer right now.

Restas: I'll bet you are. I'll bet the whole group is. You each sugar-coat your feelings. You pretend to be interested and concerned, but you don't care. You are fascinated with death.

Don't look to me to satisfy your curiosity. Keep your hideous warmth to yourself. I don't want to join the group. I don't want what you call "life." I have tasted it and it was overripe and too sweet.

Richard: You seem to be getting pretty excited. Aren't you afraid the exertion may warm you?

Restas: That is the kind of stupid, irritating remark that I hate. If you had seen what I have seen. If you had been through two wars and two totalitarian governments, you wouldn't have such a little, smug mind . . . I feel sorry for you. I feel sorry for you all. You sit there—superior, pitying, watching me suffering. I am suffering. The pain is growing . . . I should leave now. I should go to my room and get something for the pain. But I won't give you the satisfaction.

Richard: Really, Restas. I am concerned that your anger may

trigger the unfreezing process. I wouldn't want to be responsible.

Restas: You wouldn't want to be responsible! What the hell do you want? All you do is stir people up and then you step back with a picture of mock horror on your face and say, "I am not responsible."

Let me tell you, you tin god . . . let me tell you the truth . . . You are a coward like the rest . . . You are a hollow balloon . . . a caricature of a person . . . You are not real . . . Take away the group and what would you be? . . . a man caught with his pants down . . . I know you. You look good here . . . but I have seen your weaknesses. I have smelled your fear . . .

Richard: Are you feeling any tingling in your fingers?

Restas: Yes, I am. It feels like I am being stabbed by needles. Is it going to get much worse?

Richard: Probably. I don't think you will be able to take it.

Restas: I can take it, if I want to. Are you scared I will cry out? Are you scared that if anything happens to me you will be blamed? Does the real thing make you afraid, fearless leader?

Richard: I see you have found me out. I am a little boy pretending to be king.

Restas: You are naked and I have pointed the finger at you. All the others are looking now and saying, "He is just like us. He is not a god."

Richard: How does it feel now?

Restas: You know how I feel. There are steel pins digging into my nerve endings.

Richard: Ann, run into the kitchen and get all the ice they have . . . and bring back some towels.

Restas: You want to freeze me up again.

Richard: Hurry!

John: Isn't there something we could do?

Richard: What do you want to do?

John: I thought if we all touched him . . .

Richard: Do you want that?

Restas: NO! STAY AWAY FROM ME!

Richard: Easy, easy.

John: I feel so helpless, sitting here.

Richard: You don't have to be a hero, Restas. You can cry out if you want to.

Restas: I—don't—want—to. Stop trying to make me weak. Just because I showed you up doesn't mean you have to castrate me.

Richard: Nobody here will think less of you. You don't have to suffer silently.

Bill: I really wish you would scream if it hurts that much. It is hard for me to believe that it does. You just sit there.

Restas: You don't believe it. You little stupid nonentity. You should feel it for a few moments. You would get down on your hands and knees and beg for relief. You would sell your soul. You would . . .

Ann: I have the ice.

Richard: I am going to give the ice cubes to everyone and ask them to press them to different parts of you. They won't touch you, only the ice will. If it is too cold, they can wrap it in towels. Is that all right?

Restas: Hurry. Maybe it will help.

Ann: Let me try on your forehead. Is that any better?

Restas: Yes! It doesn't feel cold. It is warm. What a blessing. Yes, everybody. Do it! Cover me from head to toe in ice. Let me take off my shirt and my pants. Cover me. Please, oh please.

For five minutes the group members apply ice, moving it slowly around to leave no spot untouched. Restas breathes deeply, mutters, moans.

Ann: There is no more ice in the kitchen.

Restas: That is enough. I feel better, very weak, but better. You can stop. I just want to lie down here . . .

John: How did you know to use ice?

Richard: I don't know how I knew.

Ann: I am so thankful you didn't blow your cork. I don't know what would have happened without you.

Richard: I don't mind saying that I have had it. I would love to collapse.

Frank: Why don't you?

Richard: What I would really like is to be passed around the group.

Marcia: How?

Richard: You form a circle. I stand in the middle and then I relax and you pass me around the circle from one person to another. Then after a minute or so you lift me up, trying to keep my body more or less straight. Then you rock me. Then you slowly put me down. Then, if you want, you keep your hands on me for a minute or two and slowly take them away. Can you remember all that?

Marcia: If we forget, we'll improvise.

Richard: That's what I am afraid of. I'll have to take my chances. I am yours.

Richard is passed around, lifted, rocked, lowered. The group remains around him. Ann begins to cry. A few tears run down Thurston's face. Bill looks very somber . . .

Restas: What is happening? What are you all doing? Where is Richard? There is something I must tell him.

Richard: I am under here. What is it?

Restas: I think I am all right generally.

Richard: That is good.

Restas: Are you sick?

Richard: No, just collapsed.

Restas: Did I do that to you?

Richard: There is such a thing as a creative collapse.

Restas: Can I do anything for you?

Richard: Rest and get your own strength back . . .

Marcia: John and I want to do something for you. We want to work on you from top to bottom. We want to massage you. Get undressed.

Richard: Yes, ma'am.

Marcia: And enjoy it.

Richard: I'll try.

John: Anyone else who really wants to is welcome to join us. But if you don't feel it, please don't do it.

For fifteen minutes John, Marcia, Norma, Frank, and Thurston work on Richard. He is silent. He hardly stirs . . .

Bill: I hope he isn't dead. The weekend isn't over yet.

Sheila: Speak to us, Richard.

Marcia: Leave him alone.

Sheila: He never left us alone. Come on, Richard. How are you? Have you had enough?

Marcia: Can't you shut up!

John: Take it easy, Marcia. Leave her alone and she will stop.

Ann: I guess this is what I was afraid of—what would happen if Richard fell apart. This is worse. He isn't even functioning.

Norma: But everything is all right, isn't it?

John: I feel very good right now.

Restas: I don't know what is going on. What is going on?

Ann: The main thing is that you are interested.

Restas: Listen, Thurston. You are a man of some maturity. What is happening?

Thurston: You seem to have killed off the leader.

Restas: I didn't mean to.

Sheila: Maybe we all did. We have really been dumping on him.

Bill: But he has been working us over the coals.

Marcia: I keep wanting to tell Richard that I really love him, but that doesn't seem right. I am not after him. I don't even know who he is. But my heart overflows looking at him lying so quiet, so withdrawn, and so helpless. Maybe I want to protect him and nurse him.

Restas: Now that I am finally here, I ought to have something to say.

Ann: Do you?

Restas: I ache all over.

Ann: Is that all?

Restas: I am still very angry. I am burning.

Ann: But . . .

Restas: I feel a growing sense of gratitude.

Ann: And?

Restas: Who are you, my inquisitor? Am I supposed to recant?

Ann: My, Restas, I do believe you are paranoid.

Restas: I haven't got the energy to laugh. And it isn't funny. I was very sick. I am still sick, but the worst of it is out of me.

Penny: We are all thankful for that.

Restas: But I feel guilty looking at Richard: I shouldn't have done that to him.

John: Don't take all the credit. He is our leader, but he also is our victim.

Norma: It goes together.

Sheila: You would say that.

Bill: He isn't Christ.

Restas: And I am not Judas.

Penny: What does it matter who any of us were? We are here together.

Thurston: It seems much easier to relate to Richard, now that he is quiet. I hope that he stays that way.

Restas: I don't. It makes me nervous.

John: He is not your victim.

Restas: But I wanted him to die. He was torturing me back into life. I feel that my wish was granted.

Sheila: I remember when I was eleven years old wishing that we had more money. Then my favorite aunt died suddenly, leaving us some money. I stopped wishing after that.

Bill: What do any of us want?

Restas: If you don't know, who can tell you?

Ann: How is it without the glass wall?

Restas: I feel vulnerable but it is good to be touched by the breeze. You can't imagine how sensitive I am to your slightest motion.

Norma: Maybe we should leave him here and all go out and play. He is asleep.

Sheila: He is listening to us.

Bill: Does it really matter?

Ann: Are you through with drugs, Restas?

Restas: Do you want me to be?

Ann: Yes.

Restas: Are you through with being frigid?

Ann: Same question.

Restas: Same answer.

Ann: I wish . . .

Restas: I know—that it were that simple.

Norma: You wouldn't go back, would you?

Restas: Are you going to feel guilty about sleeping with Alan last night after you leave here?

Norma: I hope not.

Restas: But you don't know?

Norma: I am confused about the whole thing. I guess I was carried away. I hope he doesn't try to make something of it.

Thurston: Can any of us be sure?

Penny: I wish I were a little girl again. My life has got so muddied up.

Bill: I wish that I were older and were really satisfied.

Thurston: Age doesn't answer any questions.

Sheila: I don't think you really like women. They arouse you, but as people you resent them.

Bill: Stop analyzing me.

Sheila: You don't like me.

Bill: That's different. No, I don't like women who analyze me. It makes me feel inadequate.

Sheila: Only because you are.

Marcia: How about letting it alone? Can't we be together quietly?

Restas: How are we going to bring Richard back to life?

Penny: We could breathe on him.

Ann: We could tickle him.

Restas: We could sit on him.

John: What's the hurry? Once he comes back, he will be driving us again. Can't we just enjoy the peace?

Restas: I wonder how he is feeling.

Frank: Why don't we each say what we think? That is what Richard would probably suggest if he were functioning.

Bill: He is thinking, "I am really enjoying their knocking themselves out trying to arouse me."

Thurston: "I am so relaxed and so exhausted. Unless there is an emergency, I am just not going to move."

Norma: "I have given everything. I must rest and be refilled."

Marcia: "I am not really here. The voices are far away. I am in a different world."

Thurston: "What a funny group of people. They think so much. Why can't they just accept my absence and go on from there? I wish they were free of me and I of them."

Restas: "I am cold. I need a transfusion."

Penny: "I just don't care anymore. If the building burned down I would still lie here."

Alan: "This would be a good moment to die—a quick heart attack, killed in action."

Ann: "These people. They don't really care about anything. Today they are concerned. Tomorrow they will have forgotten."

John: "I exist. That is all."

Penny: Now what do we do?

John: We leave . . .

# Sunday afternoon

Penny: Is this really the last session?

Norma: I wonder how I will feel this time tomorrow?

Ann: Won't this group ever meet again?

Richard: Whether you ever meet again as a total group or in part is up to you. But it is better to think that when you leave here, the experience is over. Anything beyond today should be a new beginning.

Thurston: It will seem strange returning home.

John: We are not leaving yet. How much time do we have?

Richard: We have three hours, if we want it.

Ann: I feel so open that it scares me. Won't I be at the mercy of anyone who wants to attack me?

Richard: It isn't over yet.

Bill: What could be left?

Norma: I have had all I can take.

Richard: I am ready to start again, after the wonderful rest.

Restas: Why did you come back to life? We were having such a good time mourning for you.

Richard: Sorry about that!

Penny: What was happening to you?

Richard: I was very far away. I could hear you, but I wasn't present.

Penny: I'll bet you hated to come back.

Richard: At first I thought that I should hurry back. Then I decided to go with the experience. Eventually it ended of its own accord.

Frank: What do we do now?

Richard: I want to suggest an exercise that I didn't think would mean a great deal before, but which may be effective now. I want each of you to look at another member of the group, but not someone who is looking at you. Do this for five minutes. During all that time identify as completely as possible with the other person. Try to feel that in looking at the other you are looking at yourself. It may help to repeat the words "I am looking at myself" silently. It may also help to sense that your perceptions are part of your larger self. Everything we perceive is actually our own nerve impulses. The "other" is inside us. Try different ways, but don't think about it. Sense it. I am the other. The other is myself.

Select someone and try for five minutes. If something begins to happen to you, accept it. Don't be frightened and don't stop. If nothing happens, be patient. Start when you are ready. I will let you know when the time is up . . .

The room is almost totally silent. The group looks like a medieval painting in which no two people look at each other. There are moments of restlessness. Frank develops a twitch in his left eye. Marcia's shoulders get stiff . . .

Richard: Five minutes are up. What was your experience?

Thurston: I looked at Ann. At first I couldn't get anywhere. I kept saying "I am Ann." That was ridiculous. My mind kept denying it. Then I thought about Ann being inside my head and

I thought about all the different things I have inside me. And then for a moment something happened.

Ann: What?

Thurston: I was you.

Richard: And now?

Thurston: I have this very weird feeling as I look at her and when she speaks. It is as if I am speaking.

Ann: Then who is speaking when *you* speak, if it isn't you?

Thurston: I can't answer that. I only know that if I look around the room, when I come to you it is as if a spotlight had been turned on. You seem so much more vivid and alive than the other people . . .

Ann: I focused on John. But I must have been doing something wrong.

Richard: Why?

Ann: I just concentrated on him. I noticed different features, how his nose curves around the edge; how his ears are attached to his head. But I couldn't seem to get inside him. If I said to myself that he was I, something else would say that it was just ridiculous.

John: Was it because I am a man?

Ann: Maybe that was it . . .

John: I looked at Restas. I seemed to get right into it. I guess my sense of personal identity isn't too strong. I experienced what Thurston described, but then I began to see pictures. I saw the remains of his iceberg still melting. I saw that his skin was slightly frostbitten. I saw him out in the middle of the ocean, treading water. Then I saw him looking much younger with very somber eyes. But what was so strong was this dual sense of seeing into him and at the same time looking at myself. I understand more about him now but it is as if it were self-knowledge . . .

Marcia: I looked at Richard. I guess that doesn't come as a surprise to anyone.

Richard: What do you know now that you didn't know before?

Marcia: I don't know quite how to express it. I feel a certain awe.

Richard: What did you experience?

Marcia: Mainly light. At first it was light coming out of you. Then it was between us. I didn't become you but we both became the light that flowed between us. That doesn't sound like much in words, but I am still feeling the physical after effects.

Richard: How do you feel?

Marcia: Partially anesthetized.

Restas: What does that mean?

Richard: What do you think it means?

Restas: I am not sure I want to know . . . I looked at Norma. I thought that if I could identify with her, I could do it with anyone.

Norma: Did you?

Restas: You are not so bad.

Norma: That doesn't answer the question.

Restas: I gained much more understanding of you. I am not hostile anymore.

Norma: I didn't know you were before.

Restas: When you talked I wanted to grind you into the floor.

Norma: I'm glad I didn't know about it.

Restas: I don't feel it now. I feel warm. I would like to put my arms around you. Would you mind?

Norma: All right. Just don't change your mind and start hating me. I would rather you do that from a distance . . .

John: What does this whole thing mean?

Richard: You know perfectly well.

John: I suppose I don't want to know . . . It must mean that we could be more than just ourselves.

Richard: One form of personal growth is to expand one's sense of self. It can be done with a glass of water, a stone, a tree or another person. We have the unused power to place our identity where we wish it to be. But it must be cultivated.

Thurston: Isn't this a terribly important discovery?

Richard: It is a very old one. The ancient Indian text says, "Thou Art That." To them it meant that the small subjective individual is identical with the universal spirit standing behind the manifested universe. We are, from their viewpoint, all characters in its dream. It is a subtle doctrine.

John: What does "that" have to do with encountering?

Richard: I and thou. Encountering is not you or I, but it is the process between us that happens when we meet. There are truly no separate people. We are all bound together, much as we resist it or seek to deny it.

Frank: Do you believe in a group mind?

Richard: What does it matter?

Frank: If it didn't matter to me, I wouldn't ask.

Richard: I mean, what does it matter whether I believe in it or not? If it is true, it is true. If it is not true, it is not true. My belief is not necessary. Use your own experience as a guide. Has anything happened to you for which such a concept is necessary? So many of our problems are created for us by the concepts we use. Every structure is an abstraction which we create. The real thing, the event, is always a process. We are all flowing in a common event. The more alive we become, the more we flow.

Those are nice words. They sound poetic. You have to realize that they are literally true. When we are at our best, the barriers, tensions, and obstacles are removed. Everything takes place easily and naturally. Work consists in removing the obstacles, relaxing the tension, increasing the energy pressure so that the flow can take place.

Sheila: I always get uncomfortable when we start to talk about things abstractly. Maybe I'm not much of a brain, but words scare me. They are supposed to explain things, but they seem only to lead me away. Couldn't we have a fantasy about flowing? That would have much more meaning to me.

Richard: How would you like to do it?

Sheila: I would like to have everyone put his head together on the floor, like a giant pinwheel. And then we just start from the image of flowing water and see where it takes us.

Penny: That sounds like fun.

John: I am thirsty already.

They all lie down.

Sheila: I'll start. It is a mountain stream flowing through a small pine forest. The water is very cold and very pure. The sun is brilliant. The wind blows all the time . . .

Frank: The sun is going down. The clouds are sweeping in. It is getting dark . . . It is beginning to pour. The raindrops make big rings in the stream. They blend into the water. The stream is swelling . . .

Penny: And it comes to the edge of a cliff and goes shooting off . . . a temporary waterfall . . . The feeling of the water dropping into space is tremendous. It takes my breath away . . .

Bill: And it crashes onto the rocks below. The spray comes shooting up. The rocks groan as they rub together. They are worn smooth. And then the water moves more slowly into the lower lands. It is entering a small river . . .

Norma: It goes through farm lands now . . . the smell of wheat . . . it is not so pure anymore . . . garbage is dumped into it . . . little boys pee in it . . . but it moves along . . . the weather is sultry . . . the sun sucks some of the water up into the sky, but most of it goes rushing on . . .

Marcia: I am in the stream, a piece of driftwood . . . moving more slowly now . . . caught in little eddies . . . swept out in the current . . . bumped by boats . . . I am soaked with the water . . . the edges of the river are getting broader and broader . . .

Restas: I pass harbors . . . I pass cities . . . I am polluted . . . abused, but somewhere up ahead I will be purified. My load will be taken from me . . . so that keeps me going . . . but I feel much heavier . . . much more pressure.

Alan: I want to escape . . . but the current pushes me on . . . I struggle . . . I get becalmed . . . but I am pulled on . . . people ride on me . . . fish swim through me . . . I stir up the bottom as I flow . . . but nothing can stop me now . . . in the distance is the sea . . .

Ann: The taste of salt . . . at first hardly perceptible . . . but increasingly strong . . . It is frightening . . . I will cease to exist . . . That is what I want and what I am scared of . . . But there is no choice and no escape . . . It is far more powerful . . . than I . . .

Richard: Now, for a moment, try to see the whole stream as if you were high in the heavens looking down, able to see it from the mountains to the ocean. Experience it as a totality in all its varied forms. Experience it . . . and then . . . let it go . . . And sit up.

Sheila: It is still flowing.

Marcia: Maybe it is always flowing, but we aren't aware of it . . .

Sheila: I feel good—light and full and moving. How about making up poems? We could each make up a line. I'll start.

"The water flows softly over the mossy rock." Now somebody else.

Penny: "The fishes swimming below are startled by an unexpected stone."

Bill: "Little boys are playing in the afternoon sun."

Ann: "Their mother watches them like clover, sitting at the stream's edge."

John: "The water sings to her of quiet hours of content."

Thurston: "Rocking by the fire or in bed."

Marcia: "She counts the running sands inside her head."

Frank: "She wishes that the ancient past were truly dead."

Norma: "Her children playing in the soggy sand revive her from the past."

Alan: "And promise her of all that is to come."

Restas: "It waits. It beckons. Everything is one.

      The stream, the children, and the setting sun."

Richard: Very lovely.

Sheila: We are such a beautiful group. I don't want to leave.

Richard: We are not leaving yet.

Sheila: It has been such hell. I know I haven't said too much, but I felt it deeply. This room is an oasis. I know outside it is going to be cold and dark. People don't understand. I want to hug everybody here.

Bill: Why don't you? If you want to skip me, you can.

Sheila: I don't want to skip you, Bill. (*She moves slowly around the group, embracing each one in turn . . .*)

Richard: How do you feel now, still sad?

Sheila: I could cry very easily. I feel very full, very happy.

Richard: And all the things you know about different people here doesn't turn you off?

Sheila: No, that is part of it. It is such a relaxed feeling. There is nothing to hide. What does it all matter? The past is sad because it is so ineffectual, so incomplete . . .

Restas: I wish we could sit together quietly for five minutes. Do we have to talk all the time?

Richard: Why don't we spend fifteen minutes by ourselves. Stay here if you want to or go outside in the sun . . .


*In the sun*


(I feel cozy and complete . . . If I have a momentary fear, I can visualize myself talking about it and it goes away . . . I am protected . . . I am naked.

(I hurt inside. I have been bruised. Is it the aftereffects of surgery or just a blow? I can't tell . . . I am happy to be alive . . . I am grateful to be here . . . I am so grateful to feel that there is really a chance for me . . .

(Will it last? It can't, I suppose. And I can't try to keep it . . . Where has it all gone—the tensions, the suspicion, the confessions? Has the earth absorbed them? I cannot even remember what has happened . . . I almost cannot think . . . I am here . . . The sun is touching me . . . going into me . . . going through me . . .

(My body is quiet. My mind is a whisper . . . My personality is almost transparent . . . Nature is reflected in me . . . My sensations are surprises coming from the outside . . . from a mysterious place . . . on the first day . . . on the last one . . . unknown . . . unless it reveals itself . . .

(Mother, I can see you now . . . I am close to you . . . Your daughter whom you left behind so reluctantly . . . You need not be afraid . . . I bless you for giving me the chance to be here . . . I was always indifferent before. Life is such a mean and grubby struggle . . . It hasn't changed . . . But there is a shining, throbbing jewel at the center that alters everything . . . Do you know what I am talking about? Do you still exist? Do you remember me?

(I seem to hear you talking. "Yes," you say, "I can still remember, though I am confused. I cannot tell my dreams from your reality. Are you my daughter? I was once as young as you. Am I your mother? No more. I am a naked soul seeking its way."

(Bless me, Mother.

("How can I bless you? I am dead. It is you who should bless me with your energy."

(What is happening to you?

("That is not for you to know. All that I can say is that you must find the secret of life while living. It is there. You are so close to it. I have never seen it. From here it is invisible . . ."

(So it is I seem to speak to her . . . What is the secret? Is there a secret? I would love to believe so. Is it all a fairy tale to disguise the brutality? Is it romance sugar-coating the lust?

(It must be palpable . . . It must shine and warm like the sun, though it comes from an unperceived source, reaching me in my depths . . .

(I am so small—a particle in the vast sphere on whose circumference the sun shines. But I seem to extend in every direction. I do not end in the atmosphere. I do not end in the dark night of starlight. I flow. From every sector messages are sent, and I respond. I give back.

(Is this state some temporary dislocation? Am I near the truth or drifting away on an intense cloud of illusion? What has John done to me? What did I take from him? Why do I wish to move swiftly through space like a winged messenger?

(Why do we cripple ourselves? Why do we limp toward our

grave? I am frightened. A clock is ticking in my head very softly. I had not heard it before.

(Marcia, you think so much. Isn't it enough to be here resting in the sun? Isn't it enough to sense that you have hardly begun and that there is somewhere to go? Be peaceful. Be grateful and know that all may be well. Accept the vultures, the fungus, and the indifferent spectators. Understand the devils are driven wild with envy . . .

(I want to be purified. Lying here, I want to be filled with light. I want to suck on energy like a baby on a breast.

(Every moment the candle flickers. My attention wanders and when it returns, the light is gone.

(I am very weak. I can't contain much energy. It leaks away from me in dreams, tension, distraction. I am afraid of many things. I love many things. I am alive. This is the miracle. I pray that I don't forget it.

(Will I see John again? Will I see Richard? I must leave this place with what I have. If help comes, or friendship, or love, I will be grateful, but I cannot build my house on that foundation. I must learn to walk alone.

(It must be time to go back to the group . . .)


*Mid-afternoon*


Sheila: I have been holding something back. Everything I have said was true, but I didn't want to talk about this. (*pause*) I am going to divorce my husband.

Penny: I didn't know you were married.

Sheila: I have been thinking about it all the time. I have just decided to do it.

Norma: Why? Is he unfaithful? Do you have children?

Sheila: I really don't want to go into it.

Richard: Then don't!

Penny: That isn't a very understanding attitude.

Richard: I'm sorry if I don't come up to your expectations.

Bill: Do we have to begin all over again?

Ann: I find it hard to think about anyone's personal problems. I don't care any more even about my own. I am numb. I wish I could go away to the beach for a week.

Marcia: Is there anything we could help with?

Sheila: I want to work it out for myself.

Richard: Would you object if we tried to guess the reasons for the action?

Sheila: Not if it amuses you. Go ahead.

Richard: I would guess that you have realized that you don't need him in order to be a complete person; that you never loved him and that he is really getting in your way. I don't think he is unfaithful or if he is, that it matters to you very much. Maybe you are unfaithful yourself. None of it matters. It is all somewhat shabby.

Sheila: You really have me in a soap opera.

Richard: Is it true?

Sheila: That's for me to know and you to find out.

Bill: I think he has a mistress and your feelings are hurt. You really want to hold the poor bastard up. You didn't have the courage before because he can get violent. But now you do.

Sheila: That's quite remarkable.

Bill: You mean I am right?

Sheila: I wouldn't go that far. Don't any of the women have an opinion?

Ann: I think you are cold-hearted. You may be creative and all that, but I don't think you really like men. They are a burden.

You want to shed them. I don't think you will remarry, because you don't want to.

Sheila: That is really perceptive.

Norma: I think you are a good person. This man probably took advantage of you and you got married. But it hasn't worked out. You want your freedom.

Sheila: That is really amazing. Anyone else?

John: I think that you have three children. You have been keeping the marriage together for their sake.

Sheila: What sexes?

John: Two boys and a girl.

Sheila: But how could you know?

Thurston: It seems to me that you are a mature woman and wouldn't do anything impulsively. You might want to. Right now you feel you have decided something but when you leave here you will probably reconsider it, and decide against taking any definite step at this time.

Sheila: There is something I should tell you. But it is quite serious. I don't mean to burden you with my troubles. It is a secret. If you would rather not have the responsibility of knowing, I can keep it to myself.

Marcia: At this point I am curious, but I could stand not knowing.

Bill: If it will help, you should tell us.

John: Somehow I think that if you tell us, it will come as a real shock.

Sheila: What am I going to do?

Richard: I guess you will have to decide for yourself. Anyone who doesn't want to know had better speak up. The rest presumably are willing.

Thurston: I think that I would rather not know.

Ann: Me too.

Sheila: But you all must know. What good is it if I cannot trust you all to keep my confidence? I ask it of you as a favor. Please stay and listen.

Ann: If I have to.

Thurston: Reluctantly.

Bill: What is it?

Sheila: It is hard to say. If I could only begin.

Frank: Just begin. We will help if we can.

Sheila: Well, you see . . . Oh, I can't.

Marcia: It's all right.

Sheila: No! After I tell you, you will never look at me the same. I couldn't bear that.

Richard: You must take that chance.

Sheila: If I really must. It is that . . .

Bill: That what? It can't be that bad.

Sheila: I AM NOT MARRIED.

Bill: Then how can you get a divorce?

Sheila: I was putting you all on.

Marcia: You made it up!

John: You deserve a good spanking.

Sheila: I told you that you would never look at me the same again.

Frank: That's a very good idea. I think each of us should give her a good swat in the rear.

Marcia: We ought to throw her into the stream.

Restas: We ought to lie on her and squash her.

Penny: I think it's very funny. She had us all fooled, even Richard.

Richard: I was took.

Sheila: It might have been true. What you said about me was interesting.

Ann: Aren't you even engaged?

Sheila: Actually I am already divorced.

Frank: Who would believe you now?

Sheila: It's true. I don't care whether you believe it.

Richard: It makes me feel better to believe it. My pride is redeemed.

Marcia: I didn't know you were proud.

Richard: Of some things.

Sheila: Have you ever been fooled completely?

Richard: Oh, yes. Usually when I get personally involved.

Marcia: With women?

Richard: Yes.

Marcia: That gives me hope.

Richard: For what—that I could be blinded to your defects? That's nothing to hope for.

Marcia: I'm just kidding. I meant if you were human, maybe I could reach you.

Ann: What is it with you and Richard? Isn't John enough? You are a pig.

Marcia: You can't blame a girl for trying.

Ann: You can't blame one for getting irritated.

Bill: If you want to fight, why don't you do it over me? I would appreciate it.

Richard: That's a great idea. Why don't all the girls attack Bill! I'm not just talking. Every one of you. Up! Go get him!

Penny, Ann, Marcia, Norma, Sheila gleefully throw themselves at Bill. He goes down in a confusion of limbs.

Bill: Help! Help! I love it.

Ann: He loves it. Start tickling him.

They all go to work. Bill laughs, shrieks.

Bill: You are torturing me. Stop it!

Ann: How about all making love to him at once? That ought to be the fulfillment of his fondest dreams.

They passionately embrace him from every side. Bill tries to be everywhere, but cannot settle on any one. He gives up and sinks back into mock oblivion.

Ann: And now for revenge. Attack him!

The women turn on him like furies, punching, scratching. Bill struggles against them. He cannot get free. He is being hurt. He makes a great effort and breaks away from them. He is disheveled. He stares at them, angry and admiring.

Bill: You really are bitches. That was great!

Frank: I feel like shouting.

Richard: Why don't we all shout . . . howl . . . scream.

Pandemonium breaks loose for half a minute . . . Then everyone collapses on the floor breathless and exhausted.

Thurston: I don't think I can talk.

Marcia: You sound like an old bullfrog. I hope your wife is pleased. Maybe she always wanted a bullfrog of her own.

Restas: If I really screamed once a day it would do me a lot of good.

Penny: I am a wet dishrag. I wish someone would hang me up.

Restas gets up, picks her up and drapes her over the sofa.

Norma: I wonder what it would be like to scream while you were kissing someone?

Alan: Let's try.

They stand close, put their faces together, start to kiss and begin to try to scream. But they are breathing into one another. They turn very red until the contact is broken and the screams come out like burst balloons. They start to laugh. The laughter renews itself every time they look at one another.

Penny: Let's all form a circle and spin around.

Everyone gets up, holds hands and starts moving around to the right. The circle goes faster and faster, wilder and wilder. Suddenly Thurston spins off, trips over a chair and collapses onto a sofa. One by one the members go twirling off into space and are hurled to the ground.

Frank: That was great. How about building a human pyramid?

Restas: I'll be on the bottom.

Norma: What do you do?

Restas: Just lie on top of one another. I need someone else with me.

John: I know I am going to regret it.

Restas: Now two on top of us at right angles.

Slowly the pyramid grows. It becomes four feet high. Sheila climbs on top.

John: I—can't—breathe.

Marcia: You look good in red.

John: I'm—not—kidding. I think I busted a rib.

Marcia: That's what Adam said.

Thurston: How are you doing down there, Restas?

Restas: It feels like—a cave-in.

Sheila: I am going to get off.

They peel off. John and Restas lie unmoving on the floor.

Marcia: Maybe we should get on them again.

John: Peace. I'm not moving till the doctor comes.

Restas: Just tell the police I passed away while I was undergoing withdrawal.

Sheila: The group really ought to have a name. What would we call ourselves if we were a rock group?

Penny: How about The Boo-Boos?

Bill: How about The Dirty Dozen?

Marcia: The Angelic Stinkpots.

Thurston: It seems to me the obvious name would be The Encounters.

John: Hey man, that's great. We'll put Frank on the drums and Ann can play the electric guitar in velvet black pants.

Bill: I don't want to play the drums. I want a water pistol. I could shoot it at the audience.

Ann: How about having cans of instant whipped cream and roaming through the audience shooting it off?

Penny: And pails of water.

John: And a big syringe labeled truth serum.

Marcia: Richard could be the leader. He could wear a black jacket. On the back it could say The Goo-Goo.

Ann: What about the whip?

Bill: What about it?

Ann: That's what I want. If anything happens I don't like, I just go crack.

Restas: But who is going to play the music?

John: We can have a hi-fi hidden in the wings. We'll be making so much noise no one will know the difference.

Norma: What should I do?

Thurston: Strip.

Norma: I'm surprised at you, Thurston.

Thurston: You could be covered with sayings like "God is Love" or "Turn the Other Cheek" or "I Love Our Minister."

Restas: I could run a freak-out clinic in the halls and take care of bad trips.

Frank: We are crazy idiots.

Penny: I want to love everyone at once. I wish my arms were bigger.

John: Just reach out. We can all fit in . . .

Everyone huddles together.

Richard: Why don't we stay this way for a little? Anyone who feels anything, say it . . .

Bill: I feel Richard talks too much. We could have figured it out for ourselves.

Penny: I feel very safe.

Frank: I would like to bowl everyone over like ten pins.

Ann: I would slowly like us all to rise in the air until we hit the ceiling and then slowly come down again . . . I would like to pretend I wasn't a Lesbian.

Penny: Are you?

Ann: You said I was yourself.

Penny: Who believes what anyone says after Sheila? Are you really?

Ann: Some of the time.

Bill: Well, after what you were through, I can understand why you would hate men.

Ann: You understand, but you don't have to live with it!

John: I am touching you now. Does that make you uncomfortable?

Ann: I feel safe. No one will hurt me. That's why I said it. But I could imagine, though, all the men attacking me like the women attacked Bill. I don't know what I would do.

Richard: Would it help to find out?

Ann: I know what it is like. I don't think anything would help. I am scared of being a woman. I wasn't always, but I was so young then.

Frank: Why is it better to be a man?

Ann: That's a stupid question. You know all about me. I wish I didn't have to be me.

Penny: Who is making you?

Ann: You don't understand. Maybe Restas understands. I may not want it. Perhaps I detest it. But it is in my blood. I may have begun in fear or a reaction to fear, but now I am used to it. I am satisfied being a man-woman.

John: If you are satisfied, why don't we forget about it?

Ann: I would be happy to forget about it, but you won't forget. It's the one thing you will remember . . . I don't care what you say. It will color your reaction to me.

Richard: What is it you want from us? Do you want us to accept it?

Ann: I am all mixed up. I think I need some help.

Richard: Have you had any?

Ann: No. I have worked out my problems on my own.

Richard: That shows guts, but everyone needs help sometimes. If you don't know anyone but want to pursue it, I will be happy to suggest some names.

Ann: Thank you.

Richard: But give it a little time. Here you see with brilliant clarity things unseen before, but their relation to ordinary life may be distorted. Some things are serious but don't bother us, such as being half-dead to most experiences. If, however, we transgress the social mores, the inevitable guilt, uncertainty, and secrecy involved causes chronic anxiety. In a different world it might matter much less to whom you made love. But you know, Ann, whatever you may say, that you are the way you are partly because of what was done to you as a young girl. It is not that your present state is bad. It is immature. You know that you should have grown into something else.

Sheila: Do you prefer young girls?

Ann: Yes. I had my eye on Norma, but she got away from me.

Norma: I have been uncomfortable whenever I was near you, but I didn't know why. I must be very naive.

Ann: Maybe you are just lucky.

Norma: How could you have thought of such a thing?

Ann: You would be surprised how easy it can be. You would feel safe because I was not a man. All your training has been to be suspicious of men. It would have been quite subtle. And once it had begun as a harmless pleasure, it would enfold you. I know.

Norma: How do you know?

Ann: Because I have seduced girls before.

Bill: That is really bad.

Ann: Why would it be good for you and bad for me?

Bill: Well, I don't know. That's what guys are supposed to try to do.

Ann: In your little adolescent square world, maybe. In mine, the roles are inverted. Perhaps the two of us should have gotten together. It would have been an interesting contest.

Bill: I wouldn't want anything to do with you.

Ann: But I am a woman.

Bill: You look like one, but it is a fake.

Ann: You look like a man, but you aren't. That is our similarity. Perhaps if you acted the woman's part and I the man's, we would both be freed from our obsessions.

Bill: How could I let go with you if you were thinking of me as a woman? It would be horrible.

Ann: You seem to think that I would find you a bowl of cherries. I am not trying to talk you into anything. But if you think about the possibility, it makes sense.

Richard: Would you two sit in the center of the room and tell each other why you could never have a relationship together? Just pour out every reason you can think of.

Bill: O.K. You're a pervert.

Ann: So are you!

Bill: I like younger women.

Ann: So do I.

Bill: I would injure my manhood.

Ann: So would I.

Bill: I don't like you.

Ann: I don't like you either. You are a coward.

Bill: You take advantage of innocent girls.

Ann: Don't you, if you get the chance?

Bill: I'm afraid of you.

Ann: I'm afraid I might begin to convince you. Why don't I shut up?

Bill: You might try to castrate me.

Ann: And what would you do to me?

Bill: You are the last person in this room I would want anything to do with.

Ann: I wish I had never started to talk to you.

Richard: Now stop talking. Close your eyes. Stand up and relate in any way you wish. But don't talk, and keep your eyes shut. And most important, don't do anything you don't want to do. But don't make up your mind beforehand what you want to do!

They stand facing each other about a foot apart, motionless . . . Ann takes a small step forward . . . Bill hesitates and then steps back . . . Ann steps forward again and puts her hands on Bill's shoulders . . . He doesn't move, but he stiffens . . . Ann pats his shoulders, shifts them back and forth until they relax . . . She takes another step forward . . . They are almost touching. She takes her hands away . . . They stand there for half a minute . . . Ann blows warm air at Bill . . . He grimaces . . . He reaches out with his right hand. Suddenly he circles her neck with his right arm and pulls her closer . . . Ann pushes away . . . He lets her go . . . She stands alone, breathing deeply. She steps closer again, but keeping her hands in front of her, palms facing outward . . . Suddenly she shifts. She grips Bill around the waist, pulls him closer and lifts him off his feet . . . He laughs . . . She puts him across her knee and spanks him quite hard . . . He accepts it . . . He stands up uncertainly, looking like a little boy . . . Ann takes his hand and holds it to her right breast . . . Bill grows pale . . .

Bill: I want to stop.

Richard: What is happening to you?

Ann: It is all right. I want to stop too.

Richard: How do you feel about each other now? You both look scared.

Bill: I have been through a lot on this weekend. I haven't been very popular, but at least I have my self-respect.

Richard: What does that have to do with anything?

Bill: If I go on I wouldn't think much of myself as a man.

Richard: And you, Ann?

Ann: Poor Bill. He started to want me, but he couldn't get himself to act like a storm trooper. He had sympathy for me. That is the first time I think he has felt for a woman, if you can call me that.

Richard: But why were you glad to stop?

Ann: Because I began to realize that the words I was saying before are really true. It is demeaning to me to think that this is the sort of man to whom I might respond. I, too, have pride.

Richard: It is an expensive illusion.

Ann: I know.

Richard: Why not surrender it? Why not accept that which is? Unless you do, nothing better can ever come.

Marcia: Isn't there any end?

Richard: To what?

Marcia: To how far this process goes?

Richard: I don't think so. It is more a question of energy and strength and, of course, motivation. All these memories and tendencies are waiting underground. Under the right conditions, they emerge like a ragged army of insurgents trying to overthrow the authorities, whoever they may be.

Thurston: I am finding the thought of leaving here increasingly difficult to accept.

Norma: I wonder how I will feel when I go to bed tonight. Fortunately I will be so tired I probably won't think of anything.

Restas: I wonder whether anything will change for me?

Marcia: The thing that really scares me is that in a few days all of this may disappear. It is incredible, but it is so different. How can it ever find its way into my everyday world? I would hate to think that it might vanish without a trace.

Richard: Every relationship, when it comes to an end, is clouded with emotion and regret. We have tasted the nectar of an unknown fruit. It is rare, harmonious, wild, delicious. Forever after we may be dissatisfied. That is a risk. If you find a better way of living, you will have to revise your everyday activities to make room for it. Do you really want to do that? Or are you like so many of the kids today, basically looking for the new experience regardless of its impact on your organism? It is hard to talk about it because the thing in you which talks is so rarely the same as that which acts. Most of our difficulties come because we think we are one way. We believe our own words. But when no one is looking, or our vigilance relaxes, we act very differently. There is almost no consistency.

Do you dare to experience that condition? Do you have the strength to allow these inconsistencies to reach you where you live, and destroy the images which you have so long and carefully labored to create?

John: What about you?

Richard: One of my biggest images is as group leader. I don't think any of you know how potent this position can be. It is very tempting and very dangerous. It feeds my fantasies of omnipotence and omniscience. You all want me to be a god that you can worship. You wouldn't say so. You have too much pride, but everyone is looking for something to bow down to. And everyone fights that which might be worth bowing to. I am caught in your expectations.

This is all right up to a point. But when I myself begin to believe it, we are all in serious difficulty. When I work in a group, I am usually in a good state. The pressure forces me. But outside a group I am no better off than you. After the weekend, I have to start all over again. I have to get up in the morning and get the whole mechanism functioning, like a dancer working out. And there is no group then.

But all words matter so little. They are a very surface expression. I wish myself well. I wish you all well. We have to accept one another as we have discovered ourselves to be. We have to hope that opportunities exist for better things and that the growing wishes that lie buried in the sands shall be found again by those who want to look.

As you all know, I can go on this way and I probably will if you don't stop me.

Alan: Stop! I have heard enough of that stuff. What good does it all do?

Richard: It provides a little inspiration and fills in the time.

Alan: I would rather sit quietly and think about home.

Richard: Then think out loud.

Alan: Since you asked me to . . . I don't want to go . . . I want to sleep until noon tomorrow . . . The thought of doing any work is really repulsive. I am probably shot for the week . . . I hope I don't tell anyone off and get in real trouble . . . I just don't know about Norma. I hope she doesn't end up hating me . . . but what is going to happen between us? . . . I'll leave it up to her . . . But that's the coward's way . . . Maybe I'll call her in a few days and talk about it . . . I guess we should

talk while we are still here. I don't have to, but it would help me
and maybe it would help her.

Richard: Do you want to talk about it, Norma?

Norma: I was hoping I wouldn't have to. I figured it would
take care of itself. But I'll face my fate. O.K. Alan, what do you
want to talk about?

Alan: The latest quotation on Xerox. What do you want to
talk about?

Norma: The New Testament.

Alan: We're off to a good start. What do you want from me
after we leave here?

Norma: What do you want from me?

Alan: If nobody is going to give a straight answer, this is
going to be a waste of time.

Norma: I don't know what I want. I want different things.
I want never to see you again, even to forget you ever existed so
that I can slide back into the narrow-minded girl I was when I
arrived. Part of me wants to make love to you as if we were
married. Part of me sees you as a real danger, as someone who
will lead me where I don't want to go—where I will regret having
gone. What do you expect? Am I suppose to throw myself into
your arms?

Alan: You worry me. You are too much of a responsibility.
Everything is such a cosmic event for you. If you go to the bath-
room, I am sure God has to be involved. That really puts me off.
I don't blame you. It's part of what you are. But who needs it?

Norma: That's not very complimentary.

Alan: I live in a different world from you. Girls I know are
more casual. They have feelings. But they don't have so many
obstacles to overcome in getting to them. Fanatics scare me.
That's really it.

Norma: And I am a fanatic?

Bill: I figured you would pull something like this.

John: I'll begin. In a way I feel the whole thing is none of my business. So don't take what I say too seriously.

Alan: Go ahead.

John: I think it is right for you to say good-bye. But I don't think it should be final. A month from now you ought to come together for an hour to compare notes. It shouldn't be sooner. But it should happen. Maybe when you meet you will admire the wisdom of your original decision. I don't know. You are young, uncertain, like me. Give it a chance, either way.

Penny: I think what you say is lovely, John. But good-bye is good-bye. I was involved in one relationship for three years. It went on and on. We said good-bye, came together, said good-bye. It was an endless torture. Why inflict that on yourselves? Quit while you're ahead. Alan doesn't want to get married and Norma doesn't want to have an affair. So where is it? Part, cry, and smile.

Ann: Anything I would say might be viewed as prejudice. After all, I have, or I had, designs on Norma. In part I think she should preserve that which she values so highly—her virtue. Not that it is worth much to anyone else, but it matters to her. Maybe she should be a nun. Maybe I should be, though I don't think they would take me; perhaps in a monastery. But enough about you, let's talk about me . . .

Bill: I just think you've got some real hang-ups, Norma. Alan is a good guy. He probably means well by you. Stop living in the Middle Ages. You're a cute girl, but it doesn't do any good hanging on the vine.

Marcia: I ask myself, if I were you, either one of you, what would I do? Stay? Go? What's the great difference? If it's not Alan, it will be someone of your own kind, Norma. Then a family, kids, and you'll be too busy to remember any alternative.

But at the same time you are both facing a situation you would not ordinarily be in. In that sense there is something at stake. Do you have the ability to reach out to each other across the differences? You would have to change and grow to do it. From that viewpoint the relation could be important. But I know that sounds pompous.

Frank: It would be so much simpler if you had screwed her, Alan. This way you did and you didn't. Why didn't you, anyway? . . . I suppose you didn't want to get involved. I don't blame you. It wouldn't be worth it. Even she knows that . . .

Thurston: Whenever my turn comes, I feel like I'm supposed to represent the older generation and say wise, fuddy-duddy things that nobody will listen to. All I want to say, Norma, is don't torture yourselves unless you know why you are doing it. Are you willing to have an affair if you are in love? Do you know? Can you positively say no? I can't answer that one for you.

If you asked me whether you should stay clear, Alan, I think I would say yes, unless the initiative comes partly from her in the broad light of day. Why put yourself through the convolutions of her conscience? But you haven't asked me either . . . The troubles we create for ourselves . . .

Restas: You should both take drugs. It wouldn't solve anything, but you wouldn't care anymore, so there would be nothing to solve . . .

However, if you don't like that suggestion, how about talking it over with Sheila's father? It would be interesting to meet him and see what he would say about a situation like this.

Richard: Could you play his part?

Restas: It would be fun to try . . . Suppose you two visit me in my study.

Restas as Father: Come in . . . Come in. You must be Alan.

Sheila has written about you. She says you are an unusual young man.

Alan: What else did she say?

Father: Nothing really. She thought it would be better to discuss the matter in person. So what is it all about? It feels like a conspiracy.

Alan: I could be tactful or I could come right to the point.

Father: To the point, please. I am surrounded by deceit.

Alan: I think Norma wants to know how you would feel about our having an affair.

Father: Is that right, my dear?

Norma: That's not the way I would put it . . . but yes.

Father: A few details perhaps?

Norma: We met at that encounter weekend.

Father: You met. That is nice. Surely you met other people as well?

Norma: No, you don't understand. We spent a night together.

Father: Then what is there to talk about?

Norma: It wasn't that way at all. Are you just being difficult or do you enjoy my being embarrassed?

Father: You must admit that if two people, a man and a woman, spend the night together there is only one likely conclusion. What did happen?

Norma: I am embarrassed to talk about it.

Father: Come, come, my child, you know I am a part-time reprobate.

Norma: Stop treating me like a little child. Alan was hurt. He needed someone. I stayed with him.

Father: Ah. I see. You sat by his bedside and held his hand. Now you wish to know whether you should hold his other hand as well.

Norma: You are an infuriating old man.

Penny: Guess what?

Frank: What?

Penny: I feel sick.

Frank: You never could hold your liquor.

Restas: You must be suffering from separation anxiety. That's what we called it at the hospital.

Penny: Oh, that's what it is. That really makes me feel much better. Would you all mind hugging me for a little while until I feel better?

The group gathers around Penny and embraces her.

Richard: Would you like to be rocked?

Penny: I would love that!

The group gently lifts her up and rocks her for thirty seconds.

Richard: Anything more?

Penny: You're being too nice to me.

John: Why shouldn't we be nice to you?

Penny: I haven't done anything to deserve it.

Ann: Should we drop you? Would that make you feel better?

Penny: Just put me down . . . slowly . . . That's fine. I feel better . . . somewhat.

Bill: What time is it?

Restas: Quarter to five.

Bill: Don't we have to be out of here by five?

Sheila: Do you realize that that is the first time anyone has asked what time it is? Do we have to leave by five?

Richard: Yes.

Sheila: But that is only fifteen minutes. How are we ever going to end so soon?

Restas: All we have to do is say good-bye and walk away. That only takes a few seconds.

Marcia: It is hard enough to say hello. When you have said that, good-bye sticks in your throat.

Father: Not so old. At least some do not think so, heh, heh, heh.

Norma: We were in bed together.

Father: But fully clothed?

Norma: No.

Father: Partly clothed?

Norma: No clothes.

Father: All night?

Norma: Yes.

Father: And nothing happened?

Norma: We had an agreement.

Father: Young man, either you were very tired or you have extraordinary will power.

Alan: Maybe I was afraid of the consequences.

Father: Such as a shotgun wedding? The picture begins to clarify. So what do you want to know?

Norma: I want to know whether to break off with Alan or go further.

Father: And you wish me to endanger my own tarnished soul by advising you on this delicate matter? Is this Alan's idea or your own?

Norma: Neither. Actually a member of the group suggested it.

Father: He must have had a strange sense of humor. As a minister, I can scarcely urge, much less condone such shameless proposals. As Sheila's father, I must view with mixed horror and relief the designs of any young man on a young woman. But as a human being of some experience, I wish for you, my child, that it might be possible, if not with him then with another. Perhaps it would make you less sure and more wise. God does not require us to be right so much as to be understanding, and humble in our weaknesses. But if I were in your shoes, young man, I would be inclined to run. I certainly would never make the mistake of

urging her against her will. It would come back to haunt you.
Is that what you wanted to know?

Norma: I think so.

Alan: I am really glad to have met you, sir. You are quite a
character.

Father: Even my enemies grant me that. Good-bye then. I
must be about my duties, such as they are in this Godforsaken
spot . . .

Norma: Have I been wrong all these years?

Alan: About what?

Norma: What I thought was right and wrong.

Alan: What you were told, not what you thought! You are just
beginning to think now. And maybe what you will think is what
you were told. Who knows? I feel better anyway. There is
nothing hidden.

Norma: What will we do?

Alan: I think the first suggestion was the best—meet in a
month for an hour.

Norma: That is a long time.

Alan: Maybe not long enough.

Norma: You don't seem to care one way or the other. I am
scared that if it happened between us you would grow cold.

Alan: I am doing you a favor by staying away.

Norma: I don't know what I want.

Alan: In a month then . . .

Richard: The time is getting on. Does anyone else have anything to say?

Thurston: What do you think my wife will think when she
sees me?

Penny: She will be impressed. You look like Santa Claus without a beard.

Thurston: I feel more like Odysseus home from the wars.

Alan: You were. I think you probably still are.

Norma: So I tell you to keep away, and you tell me to keep away. That's really funny. If that's how it is, where's the problem?

Alan: Only in what might have been . . . the big haunting question . . .

Norma: What might have been?

Alan: We might have fallen in love.

Norma: And then?

Alan: Isn't that enough?

Norma: I don't think so. I am trying to be honest. You ask too much of me.

Alan: I am not asking anything.

Norma: I think we should say good-bye here and never see each other again.

Alan: For you to come to me, you have to change. I think you could, but you might never forgive me for having made it necessary.

Norma: Stop talking about it. I want to say good-bye. I don't regret anything and I want to keep it that way.

Alan: If that is what you want. At least it is clean. I hope you don't change your mind two days from now when you are alone in your room and your emotions talk to you.

Norma: If I do, I can overcome it. I am good at that.

Alan: I am not going to try to persuade you of anything. I feel sad but that will pass.

Norma: Don't be sad. I would probably have made you miserable with my infernal conscience.

Alan: Good-bye then . . . Is that all?

Richard: Not quite. I think you should each know how we feel about what we have just seen, if you are willing to listen.

Norma: Sure, but there is nothing more to say.

Frank: How are we going to end? I hate to just walk away.

Norma: I know what I would really enjoy.

Alan: I'm not sure I can stand to know, but what?

Norma: To begin all over again.

Alan: Begin the group again? You are a martyr.

Norma. No. Begin everything all over again.

Richard: You mean being born again?

Norma: That's right.

Bill: How corny can you get. Leave it to the evangelists.

Norma: I don't mean that. I mean starting over again. Being conceived and growing up.

Bill: That's an idea. How would you go about it?

Norma: I don't know. I thought Richard would have an idea.

Richard: With only twelve minutes to go, she wants to be reborn. Is that a trip most of you would like to take?

Everyone shakes his head yes.

Richard: I was afraid of that. All right then, lie down and get comfortable . . . Forget about everything . . . Forget that there is anything to forget . . . Relax . . . Sink into the floor . . . Be present . . . Be aware of your sensations . . . Feel like a stone slowly sinking to the bottom of a pond . . . Follow the stone all the way down . . . until it reaches the bottom . . . Then let it sit there, becoming aware of the water and the things that live in it.

          Don't stop breathing . . . Everything is dark. It is black . . . Imagine, if you can, an egg and a sperm very far away from one another. Perceive them both and also the vast space between them . . . Follow them as the sperm comes closer . . . until they touch . . . and interpenetrate . . . See the two cells become one . . . You have just been created . . . Shortly the cell begins to split into two cells . . . into four . . . eight . . . a cluster of cells . . . As you watch, you begin to see the early differentiation of nerves, muscles, skeleton . . . a body is emerging . . . it has gills . . . it has a tail . . . all the details appear, first hazy and then with greater clarity . . . facial features, eyes, nose, mouth, hair . . . Growing, growing, growing . . . Feel what the fetus feels . . . floating in the dark . . . Sense what it senses . . . alone . . . without sight, sound, touch . . . Everything is muffled, indirect, shrouded in darkness . . . There is nothing to do . . . Nothing that can be done . . . Swimming movements in the blackness and always growing, altering, differentiating . . .

You are a vital process . . . consuming, excreting, preparing yourself for what is to come . . . Begin to sense that something is to come . . . that you are waiting for the change. Not knowing what it is, but knowing that it is . . . Beginning to long for it . . . Everything is ready. You are prepared . . .

Then, it begins. The walls of your space throb . . . The water by which you are surrounded presses in upon you . . . You are moving slowly in a definite direction . . .

Sense how it feels to be born . . . Sense the drive, the pain, the uncertainty, and the longing . . . You are being torn from the darkness and from the safety . . . Far away you can sense the light . . . It is closer. You are being projected into it . . . Whenever you are ready . . . Whenever it can't be held back any longer . . . You will be born . . .

Sense the moment as you emerge . . . Sense the moment when you are free of your mother . . . The umbilical cord is cut . . . You are being held up . . . slapped . . . You take your first breath . . . You cry . . . You are being cleaned . . . wrapped up . . . kept warm . . . Soon you will sleep.

You are born . . . You are a new being . . . Anything can happen to you. Your flexibility is incredible. You are capable of growing up in any culture ever devised by humankind . . . That vast range of action is possible for you . . . It is there untouched, waiting to be developed. It is the first day . . . of a new life.

When you are ready, open your eyes and look around . . .

Penny: Where am I?

Bill: Stop the world. I want to go back.

Marcia: Everything looks so beautiful.

Richard: It is the first day. It is always the first day.

Restas: Usually when you say those things, I find it vaguely irritating. But right now, I understand. Why do we put such limits on ourselves?

Richard: We don't want the responsibility of beginning again. It is easier to drift with the tide toward death. We are born to die. The rest is an interlude.

That is the way it usually is. But what you may be able to feel right now is that death is possible in life. If you could completely let go of the memories, expectations, tensions that you drag around with you; if you could let them die, then you could emerge clean to begin again . . .

In a way, that is the purpose of this weekend—to uncover you, to unburden you, to lift you up, and wipe you clean. Now you go home to begin again.

You know, without my saying it, that you will be returning to the situations that have made you what you were when you arrived. That is your private battleground. It will do to you now what it did to you then, if you let it.

People often wonder how lasting this experience can be. It isn't meant to be lasting. It is meant to show you what vistas lie before you, even now. What you do with that vision is up to you. It certainly involves some personal decisions on your part . . . Some of you may change rather fundamentally, whether you expect it or not. I still experience the impact of things that happened in groups several years ago. Some of you may feel radically altered at the moment, but find a week from today that the whole experience has been forgotten, swamped by the tide of events in which you are immersed each day.

Whatever we have experienced will speak for itself. My words are not needed to ennoble it. One thing I should warn you of. You probably do not realize how high you are. You could easily do things when you leave here that would seem natural to you but would shock other people. So be careful. Give yourself a few days to re-enter your life. You may feel depressed when you leave. You may simply be exhausted. Be good to yourself. You have been through a very intense experience. Everyone goes numb after a while. It is only when you begin to relax and thaw out that you can begin to know what has really happened to you.

Marcia: Will we ever meet again?

Frank: That sounds so dramatic.

Richard: Do you want to?

Marcia: I was thinking what John said to Norma and Alan might make sense for all of us.

John: You mean to meet in a month for an hour?

Marcia: Yes.

Ann: Could we?

Richard: It doesn't usually happen, but if that is what you all want, I would be happy to do it as an experiment. I'll give Marcia a list of your names and addresses and leave the details up to her.

Penny: Is it 5:00?

Restas: Yes.

Penny: We have to go then.

Silence.

Penny: I don't want to leave.

Norma: I don't want to go either.

Thurston: I don't care, but I can't seem to move.

Richard: I have made so many suggestions. This will be my last. Say good-bye to each other without words.

In the darkening room the members slowly move around, hugging, kissing, crying, smiling. Finally they form a circle, stand with arms around one another for a long minute. Richard breaks the circle, walks out of the room followed by the others . . .

# An interlude
# with the author

The weekend is over. Whatever its personal meaning to the reader, it may raise a number of general questions that should be clarified.

First, is this what an encounter group is like? This is a hard question to answer simply. The preceding is intended as a written equivalent based on real events in the author's personal experience. The methods used are those which the author has either applied himself or been exposed to in the work of others.

But every encounter experience is unique. This one would fail in its purpose if it attempted to resurrect the past as I have known it. Each page and each chapter evolved from the preceding as they would on a weekend. The limitations of character are essentially those of the author, who must either utilize models of persons he has met or draw on aspects of his own personality. In reality the differences between persons, both in behavior and speech, would have been greater than portrayed.

It was clear to me as the weekend progressed that I was connected in some personal way with each of the characters gathered

for the occasion. This is natural and inevitable. The more perti-
nent question is whether you as the reader would come to take
the same attitude. In the beginning, and to some extent throughout, the weekend was approached through Marcia's eyes. But this
point of entry was broadened and finally eliminated as the weekend progressed. Any encounter experience is based in part on the
growing recognition of the need to redefine the boundaries between people and the growing recognition that what had seemed
puzzling, forbidding, repulsive, or alien in others is to be found
in oneself. Thus what begins in isolation and uncertainty ends in
the consciousness of a greater organic identity.

Those who have been through encounter weekends will have
strong opinions about the validity of this one. It will certainly not
match theirs in all particulars. It is characterized by the variety
of approaches used, the heavy emphasis on fantasy, role playing,
sensory awareness and physical expression.

Every leader has a different quality. Some are matter-of-fact.
Some encourage violence. Some are verbally oriented. Some are
charismatic and mystical. And of course many combine different
characteristics into a unique amalgam. I have presented a form
of leadership that I can project naturally into written form. The
difference between personal experience and written expression
is subtle. They are different domains, each making separate
demands.

The encounter weekend that has been described is probably
more intense than those which are available generally. This is
partly the result of the written form. If one were to describe a
half hour in which nothing happened but a mounting tension of
the participants along with their increasing frustration, it would
not be interesting for the reader. It is not too interesting to the
participants either but, being directly involved, they submit to
such phases as a necessary prelude to important events. On the

other hand, when things begin to break in an encounter group, they do so with an intensity that is difficult to capture on paper, so intense in fact that even the members cannot describe them.

This raises an issue of some concern to participants: confidentiality of information. If members share personal secrets, what assurance do they have that they will not be spread as gossip and prove dangerous or harmful to them? The obvious answer is that there can be no objective assurance that members will respect one another's confidence. The leader may agree to treat what is said in the group as secret, but he cannot make such an agreement for group members. They do not have professional codes to guide their conduct.

There are, however, several built-in protective measures. First, secrets are generally shared. After a time members know information that could prove embarrassing to everyone present. They come to have a vested interest in restricting what is said to within the group.

Second, the quality of the encounter experience is extremely difficult to transmit verbally to anyone who hasn't had it. Group members who attempt to describe some of their experiences to nongroup individuals quickly discover that they are misunderstood and unappreciated. The average person finds it puzzling or peculiar to think of a group of people standing in a circle with their arms around one another while someone tries to break into their midst. In a football game this might make sense, but why should nonathletic adults engage in such behavior?

Finally, group members come to truly care for one another. They do not gossip because they do not wish to see another member hurt. They may attack one another in the group, but they react in a protective manner to any external threat.

A second major question that ought to be clarified concerns the nature of the means employed by the group leader in directing the group. Why did he act as he did? To answer the question fully would require a detailed analysis of each of his actions. A complete explanation would require another book.

Nevertheless, it is possible to describe a number of general tactics that were employed. This may help to clarify the nature of the leader's actions.

One such tactic is *to become that which you seek to understand*. This strategy underlies much of the use of role playing during the weekend. When Ann expressed Norma's thoughts in the sauna bath, it helped Ann understand Norma more deeply. When Alan played Norma's father, it served a similar function.

In some cases a person can play himself in a changed environment to accomplish the same general end. Bill was projected into his room on the Monday morning after the weekend in order to help him gain perspective.

At a different level of experience, the use of fantasy has the same general rationale. When Richard asked Norma to imagine what it would be like to make love to Alan, he was trying to increase her understanding of an alternative for action without having to live it in reality. The birth fantasy at the end of the weekend also was intended to help people understand the possibility of rebirth by experiencing it directly.

A second important tactic that recurs throughout the weekend is to *express thought and emotion by physical action*. The basic principle is simple: identify a significant thought or emotion and express it in terms of a physical equivalent.

When Ann said early in the group that she felt on the outside of things, she was asked to physically break into the group. Later when she began to feel ill as she recalled her concentration camp experience, she was encouraged to throw up.

Similarly, when Bill began to shiver inside, he was encouraged to let it out as fully as possible. Thurston underwent a similar experience which involved hitting the couch and making loud noises. All of these methods emphasize concrete physical expression of an emotional state. The purpose of this tactic is to intensify the awareness of the state and to release some of the energy with which it is associated. Physical expression is not an end in itself, but it helps to generate heightened awareness of issues and problems that might be avoided verbally. Once this has been accomplished, a verbal approach can be more profitably employed.

A different use of the same principle is illustrated by the fighting and love-making within the group. These physical actions not only express existing feelings but open up new ones. These processes are threatening at the time. Group members may resist shifting from talk to action. But if the transition can be made, the group usually operates on a much more effective and heightened level of awareness.

A third principle involves the *recognition of multiple alternatives for action.*

All of the fantasy situations employed this principle. By expanding the definition of reality, fantasy provided the possibility of testing alternatives usually unexplored. When Norma, Richard, and Alan portrayed the scene in the woods concerning the angel, the devil, and the innocent girl, Norma was forced to face an element of doubt in relation to God that she would have avoided in other circumstances.

In quite a different context, Frank and Ann discovered something of their reaction to the group experience through the theater game involving their discovery of an unknown small object in front of them. All of the creative experiences, whether fantasy, dancing, or role playing involved the redefinition of reality in order to become more aware of its imminent possibilities.

A fourth principle widely employed involves *letting go*. Some leaders believe that this principle constitutes the core of the encounter group experience. This tactic is most clearly employed in the experiences designed to put the individual in closer touch with his physical self. For example, in the sauna the concluding moments in which Richard related the heat of the sauna to an inner purification, emphasized the need of the group members to freely give themselves to the experience.

The same approach was used on a more expressive level on Sunday morning when the group danced its feelings about the morning. This was not an intellectual activity carefully choreographed. It was a spontaneous expression of feelings through the medium of the body. It was only possible to the extent that individuals let go and allowed what they experienced to be expressed.

A fifth principle involves *becoming part of a greater being*. The first exercise on Friday illustrated this approach. The members held hands in a circle and became aware of the breathing of others and the energy that was circulating in the group. This exercise was designed to create an awareness of the organic reality of the group which was particularly striking since the individuals knew almost nothing about one another.

Many of the group activities had this quality in varying degrees. The Sunday morning dancing involved, in part, an identification with the whole. The theater game in which three people moved toward the center of the room similarly produced this sort of group identity. When Marcia sat on John's lap and received the flame which he had been carrying, a unity between them was temporarily created. The night that Norma and Alan spent together had a similar supraindividual quality.

A sixth basic strategy concerns *the directing of attention*. This tactic was most clearly employed in the theater games in which a point of concentration was explicitly stated. However, part of the effectiveness of all the exercises was that they helped to direct attention to a particular focus. If the group members had been left to their own devices, most of the experiences produced by the exercises would probably not have happened.

A seventh and final principle involves *doing something you do not want to do*. Norma did not want to go to the sauna. Ann did not want to break in the group. Alan did not want to talk about the night with Norma. Thurston did not want to talk about his walk with Penny. In a very real sense, the history of an encounter group is punctuated by persons doing things they are either reluctant or afraid to do. When they overcome this reluctance, they often experience a great relief, an upsurge of energy, a sudden insight.

Unless at some point people go against their natural tendencies, they cannot learn very much about themselves. There is a fine line between forcing someone to do something they will later regret and helping them expand the range of their action and their image of their own potential by moving them into new kinds of experiences.

There are other tactics that were employed during the weekend experience. Our purpose here is not to rationalize Richard's actions in detail but only to give some sense of the framework from which they sprang. The sources of these tactics are varied. The form of their application is manifold, but the underlying skeleton is relatively straightforward.

A third basic question that should be raised concerns the application of encounter groups within a variety of different settings. Other than as weekend experiences, what forms can they take?

Encounter groups take many forms and meet in a variety of different settings. They can meet for a weekend, a week, two weeks, nine months. They may convene without any institutional sponsorship of any kind, as in the case of the present weekend. They can be part of the on-going curriculum of a college or graduate school. They may form a part of a corporation's personnel training. There is virtually no sector of the society in which the encounter group technique has not at one time or another been applied. The results vary with the quality of the leadership, the motivation of the participants, and the clarity which responsible executives have as to the purposes which they hope to accomplish.

If the leadership is inadequate, the results reflect this failing. This seems obvious but there is some lack of clarity as to the qualifications for leading an encounter group. It is a highly diverse enterprise. No one profession has a clear mandate. On the other hand, the task is extremely complex and demanding. It must be placed in competent hands. Perhaps the most appropriate guidelines are those recently outlined by Everett Shostrom.* He suggests two levels of trained leadership. The first is the professional mental health worker: psychiatrist, psychologist, social worker, or marriage counselor. These individuals are required to meet certification standards in most states. They follow codes of professional standards and have a vital stake in the quality of the work which they perform.

The second level of group leadership is more controversial. It consists of persons trained and supervised by professionals. They must meet certain minimum qualifications such as a B.A. degree,

*Shostrom, Everett L., "Group Therapy: Let the Buyer Beware," *Psychology Today*, May 1969.

previous leadership experience (e.g., administration, teaching) and extensive encounter group participation. Only by the use of such supervised leadership can the potential demand for encounter group services be met.

The motivation of the participants is crucial. In the weekend that was described, all participants were there because they wanted to be. Though it was not specifically stated, they paid to come. The cost for such experiences generally varies between sixty and eighty-five dollars including room and board.

In industrial and work situations persons are sent by their organizations. They may not want to come. If persons come into a growth situation only because they have been paid to come, the results will be less than spectacular. In some instances, a person may have been selected because he presents problems to the organization. This may put him on the defensive and create additional difficulties.

Perhaps the most important long-range consideration in the use of encounter groups within an organizational context is that the executives must understand what is to be expected from the process.

An encounter group experience is designed to open doors, turn people on, make them more fully functioning. From the individual's point of view, these goals are highly worthwhile. But does the organization really want to develop fully functioning persons? Often such individuals cease to be docile.

They are no longer motivated by a fear of rocking the boat or a need to get ahead at any price. Thus, before encouraging individual change of a constructive character, the executive needs to be clear whether he also wishes to encourage institutional change. If he does, an encounter group experience provides an excellent catalyst. But if he does not, then turning individuals on to their own potentialities is only going to lead to conflict, frustration, and misunderstanding. In the past, there has been a failure to communicate this basic point. Individual change is not a justifiable goal in institutional terms unless the institution itself is changing. In the latter case, individual growth is an essential element in such change.

# Epilogue:
# A month later at
# Marcia's apartment

Marcia: We are all here but Richard.

John: Maybe he isn't coming.

Penny: He doesn't really want to know what has happened to us.

Restas: I hear someone.

Marcia: Come in. The door is open.

Richard: Been talking about why I was one minute late?

Ann: You just wanted to make an entrance.

Richard: Let's get started. We only have an hour.

Sheila: Why do we have to limit ourselves?

Richard: You can stay together as long as you want. But anything that should be said can be said in an hour.

Would you object to having each person make a statement about the impact of the weekend experience on his subsequent life?

Alan: That seems mechanical.

Norma: We have to start somewhere. Should I begin?

Silence.

Norma: You are probably wondering whether I have seen Alan. I wanted to, but he refused. What will happen now, I don't know. Maybe I will find out before I leave here tonight. As for the rest of my life, I have been restless. I haven't changed any of my patterns. I see the same people, go to church as often. The only thing is that I don't seem to pray for the same things. I used to be concerned about being pure and helping to enlighten the rest of the world. Now I am praying for understanding and growth. It is probably just words. Maybe it has some meaning. That's all I want to say.

Restas: I want to get this over with. I feel you are all waiting to find out what I have been up to. Am I on drugs? Have I kicked it? I resent feeling that I am on trial. Maybe you don't even care . . .

I was very high after the weekend. It surprised me. Everything around me seemed unreal. I felt very healthy, more whole than I have in a long time. Then it slowly faded. Shades of gray came into the landscape and the color slipped away.

If I said I was off drugs, I would be lying. But that isn't the crucial thing. If I said I was back where I was before, that wouldn't be true either. I didn't go to the weekend looking for a cure. I don't think I really need one. If you want to look at it pathologically, the drugs are a symptom of a deeper fear or boredom.

If I had to summarize the last month, I'd say it has been a period of restless wonder. I had accepted my life as an endless tunnel leading nowhere in particular. Now I can see it as a field, sometimes green, sometimes brown and white in the winter. I have more choice than I had before and I feel grateful for that, even though I know that it doesn't necessarily mean that things will improve. They may even get worse, but the possibilities are greater than they were before, and that is all I had the right to expect. I hope you are all satisfied, and don't view what I have said as a convenient rationalization which I have made up for your benefit. I don't really care what any of you think, in one sense. In another way, I would hate to leave here feeling that I had disappointed you. I don't feel that about many people these days.

Ann: I have a lover, a man. I suppose he isn't much of a man, but I don't want too much of a man. I don't mean to give you the impression that I have sworn off women. Why should I? I'm sorry. I feel defensive. The whole thing was very unexpected. I'm sure he is scared of women too. We are quite a pair. But I feel comfortable with him and that means a lot to me.

He was nervous about my coming here. I tried to reassure him, but maybe he was right to be nervous. Maybe I will be ready for something stronger after having talked with you. I don't know, but I feel like a little kid asking for praise. But please don't give it to me. I would only want to throw up . . .

Also, I have been having some wild dreams. I don't want to take the time to go into them, but they were brutal. Somehow after each dream I feel shaken, but better. Something is working its way out of my system. I remember the name of one of German guards. It was Hans. Not that it makes any difference. But even a rape, if it is for the first time, has some significance . . .

John: Are you finished?

Ann: I could take up the whole hour, but I am finished.

John: I haven't been restless. I have felt very, very peaceful. I haven't needed to run. Once when things were getting a little hot, I thought of Marcia and figured she could do the running for me. That was all. I was really surprised that something had changed for me. I went through the thing with Marcia in the group, but I didn't exactly believe it meant anything. It did. I am free of that responsibility. But for what? I have been wondering about that quite a bit. It feels good to stop running, but you can't make a career out of it.

I talked to Marcia once, but it was casual. I think we both felt that if there was something, it should wait until we met here . . .

Marcia: It hasn't been peaceful for me. I don't run. That isn't my thing, but I am burning up inside. The nearest thing I can think of is a thick homemade soup that you leave simmering for a day. Except for me it has been a month. I am not the girl you all met. I don't say that with pride. I don't know if I am better. I know that a lot of my adolescent illusions are getting melted down. I wonder what will be left.

But I don't regret anything. Sometimes, twice actually, I have felt lifted way up. When that happens I begin to see the landscape of my life. It looks very different than it did before. I don't even know if I'll get married. Not that that is such a big thing, but before I accepted it as inevitable.

You all look different to me than before. I can see the temporary glow produced by being here together. Then underneath I can see you as you are. Some of it isn't so pleasant. What I knew in my mind I can see with my eyes: the lust, the fear, and the uncertainty. I wish I didn't have to see it. It changes my feelings, makes them less positive, but more real. I still feel for each of you and for the group, but I don't have great expectations. It is much harder to change than I thought and the price is greater. I doubt that most of you would want to pay it, or would even get the opportunity.

I hope that I don't sound judgmental or cold. I certainly don't want you all to dislike me. I am still a young girl underneath . . .

Bill: I have been looking forward to this meeting. I wanted to tell you all about Jeanne. She is French. I met her three days after the weekend. I wanted to tell you because I was proud of myself. I wanted to boast. I wanted you to know I made it with someone, that I wasn't really a creep. But now that I am here it all seems childish . . .

I have felt a lot of hate for some of the things that were said to me. I have had a lot of fantasies about having you all at my mercy and what I would do to you. Usually I was merciful in the end. But it was *my* mercy that I granted. You gratefully received it. That seems childish too.

I have been sleeping better than I used to. Of course I am not alone now . . .

I don't know what I want to say. Seeing you all here, I don't know why I was so angry or cared so much about what you said to me. I'm sure you didn't think of me. I didn't bother you, but you sure got to me. It was like hearing a gang of kids talking about you behind your back. That is the hardest thing to forget. But all in all it has done me some good. I don't like you for it, but I guess I needed to grow up . . .

Alan: Speaking of growing up, I have been doing a lot of thinking. This thing with Norma has been ticking away. I hope we just walk away from each other tonight and forget the whole thing. It would be so much simpler. But I am afraid Norma doesn't want that to happen. If I could only pass her off as an immature nut, it would be a relief. But if she starts to open to me, I can't just walk away, even if I want to. And maybe I am an idiot. Maybe there is something beautiful waiting for me. That would scare me too. So for me the last month has been a time of waiting. Some interesting things have happened. But they don't really matter.

Sheila: I have seen my father. He was very interested in the group. Maybe he'll sign up for a weekend. He wanted to meet Norma . . . We had a long talk about a lot of things, about his life, about God, about our relationship. The one thing that really concerned him was that he had done something which had turned me off God. He said that he would rather that I hate him and love God than the other way around. That's a crazy thing for a father to say. I've always loved him, my father, I mean. I didn't care what he did. If he had been a robber I would have loved him. God was irrelevant. That hasn't changed. The whole religious thing is just background. I don't want to go through life as a minister's daughter. I don't care about that. I have nothing to prove or disprove. He picked that life for himself. Maybe it was a mistake. Maybe it was inevitable. But I don't have to affirm or deny it.

That's what I told my father. I think he accepted it. It made him feel less responsible for my lack of interest. He has enough people to carry on his shoulders. I can at least relieve him of carrying me and give him the comfort that someone close to him understands and accepts, even if she can never entirely approve . . .

But my own life is the same. There may be something happening that I can't see. I honestly don't know. I like you all but I don't feel involved with you any more. I would enjoy meeting again, but if it never happened, that would be all right too. I am probably more outside this group than anyone else . . .

Frank: I have gone back to school. I am still working at the old job. But after the weekend I felt dissatisfied with that. So I have gone back. I told them it was for advanced work. That is partly true. But I wanted to take some really different courses. This may give you all a big laugh, but I am in a modern dance class. I don't know if I will stick it out the whole term, but it is quite an experience. There are five men and twenty women.

Let's see, what else? I met an old friend I hadn't seen in a year or so and he said I am looking different. I don't know whether that is the weekend or not.

I have thought about you all more than I expected. In the middle of work some incident would come back to me. My boss noticed and criticized me for dreaming on the job. I wasn't dreaming. I was reliving. You probably wouldn't think that anything like that would happen to me . . . That's all I want to say.

Thurston: I have been shaking my wife up a bit, taking her out dancing and things like that. But she seems pleased with the change. Next time she wants to come with me on a weekend. I keep telling her that she might cramp my style and she says that is why she wants to come.

I don't know how I look, but I feel ten years younger. I really do. I hope it lasts. I was in sad condition when I came. I didn't realize it then. It has been hitting me since. There was nothing exactly wrong, just the erosion of age. It isn't very profound but I am happier than I was, and I intend to stay that way. If something good can happen to someone at my age, it can happen to anyone . . .

Richard: For me this period has been one of hard work. I have run another weekend. It is hard for me to separate the effects of the two experiences.

I suppose the main thing that has hit me is how important what I do in between weekends is. I can't just coast. Even if I can get away with it, in the long run I am burning up my reserves. So I have been working every day doing different exercises.

I spent an evening with Marcia. She didn't mention

it. I don't know why. It was important to me. I am interested in her, partly as a woman but partly as a phenomenon. I am fascinated by what is happening to her.

I was reluctant to say anything about it. I was afraid that all of you would be resentful or jealous, or misinterpret my actions. That was why I felt I had to mention it. There is nothing to hide. I hope that Marcia isn't hurt or angered by my talking about it . . . I still feel a little evasive. Also a little reluctant to pursue it further without her participation.

I felt ambivalent about coming here tonight. I was curious. I wanted to see some of you, but I was reluctant to start the whole thing over again. It is too much like reopening an old wound or celebrating the past. But I was wrong. This was a good idea. I am glad to see you all. Even if I don't entirely sound it.

You know what it must be? I get to feel confident that what I am doing has good results. But something in me isn't entirely convinced. It doesn't want to know the truth . . . But the truth seems pretty good . . .

I see that this took longer than I thought. The hour is two-thirds gone. It strikes me that there are two pieces of unfinished business—one concerns Alan and Norma; the other, Marcia, myself, and John. I don't want to get into anything extended. But it would be good to let each of these people say something to each other in front of the group, if they are willing.

Norma: I would like to. Is that O.K., Alan?

Alan: I don't want to, but I will. What's going to happen, Norma?

Norma: What do you want to happen?

Alan: I don't want to marry you.

Norma: Who asked you?

Alan: I know. I just sense that is what you would try to force me to do.

Norma: I haven't seen you in a month and all you can say is that you don't want to marry me. That's pretty ridiculous.

Alan: If you didn't make me nervous I would be happy to see you.

Norma: Do you want to see me again?

Alan: It's going to be awfully hard to be casual.

Norma: Why do you make so many difficulties?

Alan: I don't want to get hurt. I don't want to hurt you. And I don't want to get caught up in your crazy ideas of morality. They are all right for you. But not for me. I don't need those hang-ups.

Norma: You just want me to do things your way.

Alan: That would be nice, but unlikely. No, I don't want that. You are so young. If you were my kid sister it would be fine. There wouldn't be any problems.

Norma: Doesn't it mean anything to you that I am here?

Alan: It means that you like me and want some kind of relation on your terms.

Norma: Are you so sure?

Alan: About what?

Norma: That it has to be on my terms.

Alan: Doesn't it?

Norma: I don't know. I am not being coy. I don't know. Perhaps it does. I won't know unless I see you. I would like to find out. You know me well enough to know that isn't a come-on. I can't help what I am. But I don't entirely know what I am, Alan. Isn't that enough?

Alan: I suppose it is. I feel uncomfortable about it. But I am willing to go a little further down the road. Then we can see. Maybe it is all a big mistake . . .

Norma: That is good enough for me . . .

Richard: Marcia and John. Our turn.

John: I have an interest in what is happening to the two of you, but I don't really have to know about it. I haven't seen Marcia. I figured it would happen. But so far it hasn't.

Marcia: Anything between us was finished on the weekend, John. Beyond that there was only friendship. I think I understand you very well, much better than before. That makes the necessity of seeing you much less for me. Richard I don't understand. Some of him is clear enough, some is childishly open. But the essential quality eludes me.

Richard: If I were out to have an affair with you, it would be simple. But if that were the point, you could have had one with John. It would be more natural. So what is it? There is a kinship, not because of what you were, but because of what you are becoming. What concerns me is not to shut John out. He has unloaded his burden. He hasn't decided whether to take up another. I feel involved in that decision. I don't want any relationship between us to interfere with him.

Marcia: I am glad you said that.

John: Nothing is going to interfere with me. I have thought about the two of you. I have thought about the group. I have seen myself going through life as I am. I don't want it. I would be bored. I need something else, something difficult, continuous, something to get my teeth into. I knew that this interval was just a rest. I wasn't built for resting. I was built for running. But before I was running as much *from* as *to*. If I start again, I want it to be toward a goal. Don't be so worried, Richard. I appreciate your concern. I am glad you are there to help Marcia until she has her bearings. I didn't expect to be any closer to her than I am. She did the important thing. She took the fire from me.

Richard: Maybe the real reason I didn't want to come tonight was because I didn't want to hear what you would say. But it was nothing to be concerned about. You taught me something.

Marcia: So now, Richard, you can relax with me. I don't want anything from you that you don't think you should give . . .

Restas: It is six o'clock.

Richard: Then let's say good-bye.

The group slowly departs. Norma and Alan leave together. Richard stays behind.